C000152812

*To the cause of all human and
non-human awakening, everywhere.*

*And to all friends in the Climate Psychology Alliance who,
while addressing the problem of denial, are exploring our
conscious and unconscious feelings about climate change.*

EVERYTHING AND NOTHING

Essays on climate change and cultural transformation

TONY CARTWRIGHT

First published in 2022 by Vital Press

Copyright © 2022 Tony Cartwright

All rights reserved. No portion of this book may be
reproduced in any form without permission from the publisher,
except as permitted by United Kingdom copyright law.
For permissions visit www.thetimelessaxis.com

ISBN 978-1-7396676-0-3

Book design and typesetting
www.concisedesign.co.uk

Western dharma

Dharma is an important concept in Indian thought. In the Hindu tradition it refers to the cosmic truth or law underlying the universe, and in Buddhism it also refers to the Buddha's teachings, known as *buddha-dharma* which, historically, spread from India across the whole of the Asian East in the first millennium CE.

Gautama Buddha's ethical and practical teaching in the 6th century BCE is often referred to as "the first turning of the wheel of dharma". In the history of Buddhism it is also taught that there were two further "turnings" of the dharma wheel: the second, in the second century CE, focused on the teachings on "emptiness" – in Sanskrit, *shunyata* – associated in particular with the sage, Nagarjuna; the third turning was the consciousness teachings of Asanga and Vasubhandu, of the "mind-only" school – *Yogachara* – in the fifth century. It is thought by many that, with the spread of Buddhist ideas in the West, we are now living in the midst of a "fourth turning". This is a global phenomenon, not just a challenge for Buddhism.

It could be said that the quantum revolution in physics at the beginning of the twentieth century has contributed towards a "second turning" in our understanding of the Universe, and the interest today in neuroscience and mindfulness resonates with the profound teachings of the mind-only school. If the challenge of Western natural science and the West's social and political awareness constitutes a possible "fourth turning" for Buddhism, then equally, with the ecological crisis and mass extinction happening now across the Planet as a result of our modern way of life, we desperately need a spiritual infusion from the profound ethical, philosophical and psychological traditions of the East.

See also my personal website: **www.thetimelessaxis.com** for further writings on this theme.

Contents

INTRODUCTION
Global Warming and
Everything and Nothing

The five essays here were written originally for the UK Climate Psychology Alliance (CPA) which I joined in 2012. It had been recently formed by a small group of psychologists, psychotherapists and social thinkers to explore the mental health implications of the climate emergency, including: the effect on us emotionally and mentally of climate change; the widespread resistance to acknowledging it; and, of course, the crucial importance of acting to avoid it. The essays were written to help clarify my own thoughts about the cultural issues accompanying climate change. Three were posted on the CPA website but two weren't because they were thought to go beyond the aims and goals of the CPA. They drew on perennial and mystical wisdom traditions that were, then, felt to lie too much outside the focus of the Alliance.

I have been writing a book about the cultural implications of climate change and global warming for over ten years and am only now coming to an end. Conclusions are difficult where climate change is concerned. However unanimous the science has been for some time, public awareness is slow to respond and the growing literature on waking up to the fact – and the meaning – of climate change has, as it were, only just begun. Some think it is now too late, and those of us who want to keep an open mind about avoiding total devastation are finding it more difficult to do so.

The future

Earth scientists are clear about what lies ahead this century if we do nothing to curb our carbon emissions and change our consumerist way of life. The gravity of the crisis for all life on the planet, including ourselves, cannot be overstated. There are a growing number of books now on what has been named "the Anthropocene". Earth scientists maintain that, so far-reaching are the changes we have made to the Earth – not just to the atmosphere but also to the lithosphere, hydrosphere, and biosphere – that we can now speak of a new human-driven geological epoch – the Anthropocene – succeeding the stable and clement Holocene of the last 11,000 years that has made human civilisation possible. Had we not disturbed the Holocene, perhaps we could have enjoyed some tens of thousands more years before the next ice age, potentially giving us time to learn ways to steward the planet responsibly and evolve with nature rather than in conflict with it.

Yet the idea of the Anthropocene is not just the domain of the geologists and natural scientists. Now it has also captured the interest and imagination of the human sciences and the arts. The climate emergency we face raises perennial philosophical and existential questions we in the modern world have long since been disengaged from. Collective responses to our "end times" – the end of human civilisation as we know it, even our extinction – may be akin to the reactions of an individual person suffering a terminal illness – initially shock, grief, anger and/or depression before, hopefully, some understanding, acceptance, and insight – even transformation – follow.

Questions

If we challenge ourselves to think about these issues and

the changes that the scientists say are coming we may find we are asking basic questions of ourselves while we are still here to ask them, such as: what is wrong with the world, or our attitude towards it? What is the meaning of life and existence? Who am I? Who are we? What is my/our true nature? If we really think about these questions we may come to feel and see that we are not who we think we are, and that, as many have pointed out before us, the world as it appears is not the world "as it is".

These are the questions that all the mystical traditions have always asked and the emphasis has been on the questions rather than the answers. They say the trick is to ask the right question and the answer will come of itself. This suggests that the universe is essentially a great question mark, a riddle, enigma, a mystery, as are we who have emerged from it. Finding ourselves here, we begin to ask "Who are we?" There is no answer to this other than that we are of the same substance as the universe from which we are born.

Some suggest that, despite the ecological crisis we face – or perhaps because of it – a new axis of thought and experience is opening up for us beyond the material bipolar existence of subject and object, time and space, life and death, or nature and culture as opposites in our modern way of thinking. This is not an alternative to our instinctive dualism but an axis that gives it a new context. It is the continuum between ourselves and what seems "other", known in the East as a "nondual" reality.

On the one hand, for instance, we are not the separate, special and exceptional species we take ourselves to be. On the other, the climate emergency invites us to awaken to our shared identity with all around us, even as we seem to be at the point of saying goodbye to it. Perhaps if we had known this all along we would not be facing the crisis.

It is possible we are entering a period of heightened consciousness and cultural evolution akin to, but more momentous than the intellectual and spiritual illumination experienced across the world in the mid centuries of the first millennium BCE, when the history of our current civilisation was founded, and which the German philosopher, Karl Jaspers, identified as "the Axial Age". This was evidenced in India as the sacred writings of the Hindu *Upanishads* and the teachings of Gautama Buddha, in China as the taoist tradition of Lao Tzu and Chang Tzu, in Palestine the wisdom books of the Old Testament prophets, and in ancient Greece the philosophical insights of the pre-Socratics.

We may be entering a new Axial Age and, despite or because of climate change, becoming conscious again of a timeless axis, this time two and a half millennia on.

The essays

I wrote these five essays over a period of two to three years, the first in November 2015, the other four in 2017-18. Here they are in chronological order. The theme of "Everything and Nothing", the first essay, – and the title of the collection – occurred to me after reading the philosopher, Jonathan Lear's book, *Radical Hope*, about how the North American Indian Crow nation survived the loss of their way of life when the buffalo were wiped out and they could no longer do battle with the Sioux, their traditional enemy. The CPA took Lear's book as a focus for a study day earlier that year, 2015, to discuss how we might define radical hope for our own modern scientific culture, given that many people are feeling increasingly hopeless in the face of worldwide ecological degeneration. The Crow themselves had initially felt they had nothing to look forward to. They were peering into an abyss.

I take Lear's idea of radical hope – as opposed to simple optimism – as a starting point to discuss the theme of "everything and nothing" from different perspectives. In her book about climate change, *This Changes Everything*, the American writer, Naomi Klein, suggested all we have to do is nothing – to reduce global warming – and catastrophe will follow, although there is another way of looking at this. One view might be that we simply have to stop doing the things that have caused the crisis in the first place. This, it would seem, is easier said than done. It may require subtle and fundamental changes in the way we think and live. I explore what the ageless wisdom from the Eastern traditions might have to offer

For instance we feel there is something ultimate about the present crisis, as if it were an everything or nothing choice. We either survive or we don't. But perhaps it's not such an absolute either/or. I have tried to suggest that "everything and nothing" are not opposites but perhaps key to the understanding of each other. The notion of nothing, or emptiness – *shunyata* – that is central to Vedanta and Buddhist thought, is not a vacuity, as we think of it, but a fulness. In this view "nothing" – or no-thing – is where "everything" comes from. I have always wondered, for instance, how the prodigious natural life of a tropical rainforest or the sheer infinite throng of human life in any of the world's megacities emerged from the "emptiness" of space.

The second essay continues these ideas around the theme of "Awakening". I discuss two kinds of awakening which are essentially related. First is the crucial waking up to the fact of climate change and the need to face up to it. The second is awakening to our responsibility for the crisis and asking ourselves how we have caused it, which may then lead into thinking and enquiring about ourselves – our essential nature in contrast to our conditioned human nature. The mystical or introspective traditions have always affirmed a larger, more inclusive, even cosmic Self, which is host and context to the personal self. Experience of this Self is key to essential awakening. Climate change is then the cue and opportunity.

"Where has Truth Gone?", the third essay, is a book review. 2016 was a remarkable year and the three books chosen were an immediate response to its events. Naomi Klein's *No Is Not Enough* draws on all her previous work in explaining and analysing the phenomenon of Donald Trump. Her descriptions and narrating of the facts are quite shocking in themselves. The same may be said about Pankaj Mishra's

Age of Anger, except that this is a compelling literary and cultural analysis of the roots of the present malaise of the modern West from someone with a Far Eastern perspective and an awareness of the suffering and degradation experienced in the "developing" world. Mishra wrote much of his book prior to Trump's election but published it after, and is, therefore, able to comment on this in passing.

The third book in the review is Ken Wilber's response to Trump. Wilber is an uncommon writer in that he has always taken the perspective of the perennial philosophy, as he did in his first book, *The Spectrum of Consciousness*, published in 1977. *Spectrum* was a profound challenge to the psychological, philosophical and scientific establishments and he has followed it with some thirty books, expanding and developing his original ideas up until today. He is well known and respected in alternative traditions but is not readily acknowledged or cited in academic circles, despite his influence in them. His *Trump and a Post-Truth World* provides a cultural analysis of the US and the world from the widest philosophical and political perspective.

The last two essays focus on our individual and cultural identity. The growing interest in the Anthropocene, which supersedes the Holocene, raises all sorts of questions about our future. Some scientists, believing we – modern scientific man – have become a geological force in our own right, are very proud of this, as it attests to our power and technological know-how, and they seem confident that the ingenuity we have for geo-engineering can overcome all our problems. Others, particularly in the human sciences, warn that the advent of the Anthropocene casts a huge shadow over our future.

Whatever the future brings, despite or because of the uncertainty, we have an opportunity – and a need – to consider what it means to be a human being and a human species in this 21st century. "Who Are We?" explores the possibility of a new awareness and a new understanding of the self while we are still here to think about it, drawing on the philosophical and psychological understandings of Far Eastern traditions in comparison and in concert with Western psychology and social thinking.

The final essay, "The New Axial Age", explores the idea of cultural evolution. The original teachings of Gautama Buddha, for instance, were essentially practical and ethical. They are thought to have been "the first turning of the wheel of dharma". ("Dharma" in both Hindu and Buddhist traditions implies universal truth). But, as I describe in the foreword, "Western Dharma", there were two further turnings of the dharma wheel in the first millennium CE, which went beyond pure ethical teachings to understandings about the "emptiness" and interdependence of all things – including ourselves – in the second turning, and to teachings on the nature of absolute consciousness in the third.

A growing number of people believe, despite the ecological crisis we face, we are at the beginning of a fourth turning today, which is about the integration of our modern natural and human sciences, as well as our own historical religions, with the perennial philosophy of the world's timeless wisdom traditions – not just Buddhism, though the latter's impact on the modern West may come to be seen as one of the most significant events of the twentieth and twenty-first centuries.

Common themes

I also emphasise the importance of values throughout all the chapters. Take science, for instance. Although it places a premium on the importance of research and the collection of more and more data, do we not also need to restrain and challenge the orthodox scientific fixation on the accumulation of factual knowledge for itself, as if all we need is to know just a bit more in order to solve all our problems? Instead we might do well to focus back on values, particularly the three central value spheres of the Good, the True and the Beautiful – ethics, science and aesthetics. These three could be viewed as a unity once again. For example science – or the search for truth – must be ethical, or it is likely to become an instrumental scientism. At the same time the universe can be viewed as a sublime continuum – it is absolutely, beautifully and dissonantly sublime – and science is an exploration of that sublimity. Is not science also a supreme art?

Again, we – the human species – are potentially an integral and living part of the continuum. The wonder of science – natural and human – and the imaginative arts are all the more extraordinary when we contemplate the fact of the human animal – ourselves – practising them.   Darwin expressed the truth of biological evolution – his famous "endless forms most beautiful and most wonderful" that comprise "the grandeur of life", as he wrote in the concluding sentence of *On the Origin of Species*. Perhaps it is time, in this postmodern and deeply disturbed age, we realised the truth and grandeur of cultural evolution, that, despite modernity's skeptical view, the human mind – and its passions – are equally one of "the beautiful and wonderful" forms. Truth – and human nature – evolves.

The common theme of duality and nonduality

William Blake wrote that "without contraries, there is no progress", which appeals to our Cartesian mind-set, but he was also aware of the "marriage" of opposites. Body and soul may be different but they are not separate, since the "energy of delight" flowed through both, just as also "heaven and hell" were joined, in Blake's mind, as a continuum. Descartes' contemporary, Baruch Spinoza, also pointed to the unity of apparent opposites in suggesting that mind and matter, for instance, are two attributes of the one substance, which Spinoza thought of as "God".

This alternative, or contextual, axis to duality, known as *advaita* – "not-two", nonduality – in the East, was alive in our poetic and philosophical traditions. I have already mentioned Blake and Spinoza. The 2nd century, philosopher, Plotinus, conceived his axis as "the One and the Many" – unity in infinite diversity – a Neoplatonic principle that has influenced European history and thought throughout the centuries. The uni-verse is a great unified work of art which finds its expression in the Many. The Chinese thought in terms of "the one and the ten thousand things", which for Blake was "the world in a grain of sand", and for the fourteenth Dalai Lama, "the universe in a single atom".

Global awareness

One of the essential features of any new enlightenment is global consciousness, not the simple idea of a globalised economic order but a new sense of the unity of the whole universe and all things in it, evident on the smallest of scales as well as the largest – in the microcosm of daily life as much as in macrocosmic dimensions. Science has often thought in terms of a centre to the universe. Perhaps we need to realise there is no one single, universal point of convergence but to retain an openness to the truth that the centre is everywhere.

Global awareness today implies the notion of One Earth. This points to both an acceptance of a geopolitics that goes beyond the historical and capitalist Eurocentric and North American position of the modern West and a realisation that the model of the ancient Greek polis may no longer be the exclusive blueprint for the governance of the whole planet. The philosophies and world views of non-Western countries, particularly in the historical traditions of the Far East, for instance, may have a depth and breadth that give a universal and timeless context to modern Western cultural traditions. It is less a question of one being more adequate than another but of a new integration of them.

At the same time a global and integral awareness works across the whole spectrum. No longer is it sufficient to be an "expert" in a specialised area. What is needed today is also a willingness to test how expertise in one area can relate to, and transform, knowledge in another. It is questionable whether a particular speciality, and its specific technical language, is sufficiently adequate until it has been tried and tested in regular dialogue with others.

January 2022

Everything and Nothing:
Radical Hope and Climate Change

> When the buffalo went away the hearts of
> my people fell to the ground and they could
> not lift them up again. After this nothing
> happened.
>
> **Plenty Coups, chief of the Crow nation**

Quoted in Jonathan Lear's *Radical Hope: Ethics in the Face of Cultural Devastation*

In the *Guardian* newspaper of Saturday, March 7th this year (2015) there was a special cover with a single quote in the top right hand corner. The quote was from Naomi Klein's

Introduction to her book, *This Changes Everything* (2015):

> We know that if we continue on our current
> path of allowing emissions year after year,
> climate change will change everything about
> our world. And we don't have to do anything
> to bring about this future, all we have to do
> is nothing.

Alan Rusbridger, who, after twenty years in charge, was retiring as editor of the *Guardian,* wrote – in the same edition – of his intention to foreground the subject of climate change in the paper before he went. Journalism, he said, usually writes of events that have happened and ignores the future since it is unpredictable and uncertain. But, exceptionally, one possible future is very predictable. And it is explained by three simple numbers. Quoting from Bill McKibben – in July 2012's *Rolling Stone* – Rusbridger reminded us of them:

> **2C** – 'there is overwhelming agreement
> that a rise in temperatures of more than
> 2C by the end of the century would lead
> to disastrous consequences for any kind of
> recognised global order.'

> **565 gigatons** – McKibben believes we can pour 565 more gigatons of Carbon Dioxide into the atmosphere by mid-century and still have some hope of staying below 2C.
> **2795 gigatons** – this is the amount of carbon dioxide that would be released from the proven fossil fuel reserves that we are planning to extract and burn.

McKIbben, who warned us about *The End of Nature* some 25 years ago, wrote in the *Guardian* on the Monday following Rusbridger's declaration, of 'a sea change....as the confidence in the old order starts to collapse'.

Given that our past track record suggests we are unlikely to stop the powers that be from extracting and burning fossil fuel reserves well over the 2C limit and that scientists now think we are heading for 4C+ sometime this century, **I would like to make the case for "doing nothing".** I have been thinking about this since the Climate Psychology Alliance (CPA) day in June last year (2014) at the Conway Hall in London. In the afternoon David (Wasdell) gave a summary of his *Apollo-Gaia Project*, presented in March 2014 to the Climate Challenge Conference convened by

Climate Change Solutions in the I-Max Theatre of the Millennium Point in Birmingham, and gave us a copy of his paper, "Sensitivity and the Carbon Budget. The Ultimate Challenge of Climate Science", to take home. I wasn't able to follow all the science at the time but was left with a strong sense of the hopelessness of the task, so much so that I failed to make any contribution to the discussion that followed at the end of the day about what we should do as a group in future. Was there really anything we could 'do'?

The source of everything

By "doing nothing" I don't mean an idle or despairing, hopeless nothing but an active, thoughtful, contemplative "nothing". In our Western, industrious culture doing nothing often connotes something empty and vacuous, an idleness associated with a moral lack, an absence of virtue and purpose. But we know in our psychotherapeutic culture that holding back on our wish to act – doing nothing in the sense of not acting, just being there – especially when faced with extreme distress and suffering, can sometimes be the most therapeutic – if often the most difficult – "intervention", for, along with compassion, it offers the support that allows a person to draw on their own inner resources.

In the East Asian cultures, "nothing" – or "nothingness" – is highly valued since it is seen as the source of everything. "Nothing", in this view, is not the opposite of "everything", everything comes from nothing. Ironically, science knows this because it believes the universe began from nothing with the Big Bang, something that was also understood by the writers of Genesis, the first book of the Bible – interestingly scientists are now beginning to wonder about the nothing that produced the Big Bang.

The central sustaining reality of Buddhism is shunyata – *sunyata* in Sanskrit. It is often translated as emptiness. This is not an empty but a full and infinitely rich emptiness – an emptiness from which everything emerges, what in the Zen tradition is known as the ever present "origin", an origin both in and beyond time, space, and causality. In us it is experienced as the empty or original self. Again, it is not the opposite of the personal self but its source and host. In returning to nothing we are returning to our origin. This is not to discount action or recommend a secluded life apart from social and political commitment but to suggest that an active life can be enhanced by periods of quiet and focused contemplation. "Climate warriors" like McKibben and Klein are to be admired for their energy and thinking, but is

21

hope and optimism alone enough? Klein shares McKibben's belief that the climate emergency is also an opportunity. McKibben says we won't defeat the fossil fuel corporations with rational and ethical arguments alone. This will be a fight and "like most fights it was, and is, about power". Their power lies in money and can buy political favour while "our power lies in movement-building and the political fear it can instill". Of course, there is less guarantee than ever that the "movement" will win. But is not wisdom – the wisdom that comes with contemplation – the true power, win or lose?

Klein – a more recently converted climate warrior – sees the fight in terms of the defeat of deregulated capitalism and impressively links the struggle to all historical liberation movements – anti-slavery, anti-apartheid, race relations, global social justice, human and gender rights and so on. But climate change is, of course, more momentous than them all, for "this changes everything". Hers is a vision of the future that goes beyond just surviving or enduring climate change, a vision in which "we collectively use the crisis to leap somewhere that seems, frankly, better than where we are right now". Klein's title is wonderful, the more wonderful because her book cannot exhaust the meaning she – or we –

might give to "everything changing", including the change to ourselves.

"What is wrong with us?"

This is important because in one sense climate change is about us rather than the Earth. Geologists and earth scientists reassure us that, whatever we do to it, the Planet will regain its balance and regenerate without us – give or take some tens of millions of years. Mass extinctions are its means of evolution. If the dinosaurs had not been wiped out we might not have evolved. Perhaps we are not designed to survive, perhaps it's now our turn to disappear and the "opportunity" lies in what we discover about ourselves in the process. The question is whether – or to what extent – we become aware of being part of the everything-which-changes before we disappear. One wonders whether this is in Naomi Klein's mind in her interesting introductory chapter when, for instance, she writes:

> So my mind keeps coming back to the question: what is wrong with us? What is really preventing us from putting out the fire that is threatening to burn down our collective house?

The answer she gives herself is a simple one: the lowering of emissions is in conflict with deregulated capitalism, the reigning ideology. But does this really answer her question? Does this get to the heart of 'what is wrong with us'?

Again when she is writing about "the politics of human power", which is the real problem as opposed to "the mechanics of solar power" – she reflects, in the process of researching for her book, that she has come to understand "the shift will require rethinking the very nature of humanity's power..... a shift that challenges not only capitalism but also the building blocks of materialism that preceded modern capitalism, a mentality some call 'extractivism'". She concludes that climate change isn't an issue to add to the list of things to worry about – such as health care and taxes – but "a civilisation wake-up call". This comprises "a powerful message telling us that we need an entirely new economic model and a new way of sharing this planet". While one cannot but agree with her, is it purely about economics or might we ask what are the social, psychological and spiritual roots of "economics" in the first place?

While one applauds the fighting spirit of warriors such as Klein and McKibben, a reading of the current climate science, as I have said, casts a shadow over their hope and optimism. George Marshall suggests that we are just not wired to contemplate the reality of a changed climate – which is why we have done so little about it for a generation or more. In his book, *Don't Even Think About It – Why Our Brains are Wired to Ignore Climate Change* (2015), he explores the reasons why and offers "In a Nutshell" – his last numbered chapter – "Some Personal and Highly Biased ideas for Digging Our Way Out of This Hole". But in an unnumbered final chapter he offers a devastating statement about the depth of the real hole we find ourselves in – "Four Degrees. Why This Book is Important".

The difference between two and four degrees

In this final chapter Marshall sketches the reality and possible consequences that lie in store. As he reminds us, since 2008 scientists are now more willing to warn that four degrees – rather than two – is the actual future we face. He quotes Mark Maslin, professor of climatology at UCL, telling the Warsaw climate negotiations:

> We are already planning for a 4 degrees centigrade world because that is where we are heading. I do not know of any scientists who do not believe that.

Four degrees most scientists consider to be nothing less than "catastrophic" but it is a figure increasingly on the minds of senior policy makers. With details that may be familiar to many of us Marshall describes how catastrophic it will be:

- **Heatwaves** of magnitudes never experienced before – temperatures not seen on Earth in the past five million years. Four degrees is only the average, so temperatures over large land masses will rise far higher.
- Forty percent of plant and animal species will be at risk of **extinction.**
- Precipitous **decline in the growth of crops** world wide, exacerbated by drought, floods and increased weed and pest invasion.
- Total melting of the Greenland ice sheet and, most likely, the Western Antarctic ice sheet **raising sea levels by thirty two or more feet** – this would put two thirds of the world's major cities under water, as well as large regions of countries.
- **Once four degrees is reached there's no guarantee that temperatures would level off.**
- A population of nine billion will not be able to adapt to these conditions.

Professor John Schellnhuber, one of the world's most influential climate scientists, speaking at a conference in 2013 on the risks posed by a four-degree climate to Australia, said: "the difference between two and four degrees is human civilisation".

What is even more disturbing is the time we have left. "So when will we get there?" The science around four degrees keeps moving but it's possible that it could be with us by the middle of this 21st century – in our lifetime! Where, then, does this leave our hope for the future? The challenge becomes ever more urgent: how do we begin to think about climate change and its implications? This is also a question raised by Paul Kingsnorth in a thoughtful essay – "The Four Degrees" – for the *London Review of Books* (*LRB* 23 October 2014) in a review of both George Marshall's *Don't Even Think About It* and Naomi Klein's *This Changes Everything*.

'No amount of psychological awareness ...'
Kingsnorth writes out of his experience as an environmental activist for some twenty years – now disillusioned. Like McKibben in the past perhaps, he used to believe that if we just give people the information they need, they will demand

action and then the politicians will have to act. But it's not that simple, in fact it's almost completely the wrong way round. He quotes Marshall:

> Everyone, experts and non-experts alike, converts climate change into stories that embody their own values, assumptions and prejudices.

According to Kingsnorth "the real problem comes when we start trying to cram climate change into our preexisting ideological boxes." For instance, in the US climate change has been used as a weapon in the cultural war between left and right. As Dan Kahan, a professor of psychology, told Marshall, it isn't information but "cultural coding" that forms the basis of our worldviews. If you're affiliated to the Tea Party anything an environmentalist says will automatically be wrong – and vice-versa. Even people who have lived through environmental disasters often remain oblivious to the wider climate implications. This applies to us all, including Naomi Klein. Kingsnorth acknowledges the quality of her analysis and exposure of the way private capital has bound the hands of government – as well as sucking in organizations that should know better – but he also makes the point that she could only allow herself to face the climate threat when she had worked out how to fit it into her ideological box – framing her message "as a 'progressive' cause firmly aligned to the left".

Kingsnorth ends his essay by siding with the view of Daniel Kahneman whom Marshall met and interviewed in a New York cafe. Kahneman won a Nobel Prize for his work on the psychology of human decision-making. "This is not what you want to hear" he said to Marshall. "I am very sorry, but I am deeply pessimistic. I really see no path to success on climate change.... No amount of psychological awareness will overcome people's reluctance to lower their standard of living. So that's my bottom line."

Kahneman may have been pessimistic but he seems to have influenced and been greatly respected by some optimistic people, including the psychologist, Steven Pinker, and the economists, Richard Thaler and Richard Lazard. He is also admired by Salley Vickers, the psychotherapist and novelist, for his demonstration that "ultimately we are not rational" (*Observer* 16.2.2014). Kahneman's pessimism may be the result of his focus on the cognitive mind but perhaps he has also opened the door for those whose thinking takes them beyond both rationality and pessimism, including the psychoanalytic tradition of the modern West and also – I would add – the contemplative practices of all cultures.

Science and religion

Our Western scientific culture is uncommon in that science and religion are quite split off from each other. Science has rejected a divine creator but it no longer has a connection with any unifying metaphysical ground. One could argue historically that in seventeenth century Europe the emerging modern science made a pact with the Church – theoretically and practically – that it would not trespass on its religious domain if the latter would allow it to continue freely investigating the material universe. As a result science separated from religion and was able to proceed unchecked with its empirical revolution.

This may have led to the progressive achievements of the European Enlightenment but there was a downside – the development of a fundamentalist scientific materialism – and a modern material mythology – split off from ethical, aesthetic and spiritual values. It also led to the division of knowledge into two polarised spheres – objective and subjective – with orthodox science having the power to ignore – even deny – not only any metaphysical reality but the subjective experience of the human mind itself.

We see what the scientific and technological power of the 19th century Industrial Revolution led to – devastating World War in the first half of the 20th century, the development of annihilating atomic weapons, and now the actual alteration of the Earth's climate. It's almost as if the threat of our possible extinction is foreshadowed in the absence of any psychological self awareness accompanying the scientific view. Perhaps this is why we cannot bring ourselves to think about the consequences of climate change. We assume we lack the inner resources to do so.

The philosophy of scientific materialism also led to the fragmentation of our knowledge and understanding. Science used to be a part of natural or moral philosophy. But without any integrating philosophy – or world view – our scientific disciplines – natural and human – have become so dissociated they have hardly been able to talk to each other. This is the real challenge and opportunity of climate change. Has it not now become the overriding context from which all our sciences should start, the new common denominator

– or unifying thread – which could begin to integrate all our divided discourses? Perhaps it is the new meta-narrative, the common ground from which we could begin to talk to each other again, if only we could find the courage and means to face it.

Psychotherapy

This is why the initiatives of the psychotherapy professions – Joseph Dodd's *Psychoanalysis and Ecology at the Edge of Chaos* (2011) and such collections of articles as Mary-Jane Rust and Nick Tottons' *Vital Signs* (2012) and Sally Weintrobe's *Engaging With Climate Change* (2013) – are an important beginning.

Dodds considers how psychoanalysis might begin to address itself to a "Climate in Crisis" and *Vital Signs* discusses the rich possibilities of thinking about the relationship between therapy and ecology, while *Engaging With Climate Change* explores the urgent questions: why we don't engage and how we might begin to. The latter book addresses – and discusses – the complex levels of resistance – negation, denial and disavowal – and its many contributors analyse them from different social, political, emotional and psychological perspectives.

This is a challenge because of the very difficult feelings and thoughts the climate emergency evokes. In her introduction Sally (Weintrobe) also emphasizes the importance of facing up to reality as well as the need for a new ethics, an understanding of the nature of mind, and a revaluation of human nature itself.

Of course, this begs the question of what we mean by reality – or the Real – and how our understanding of mind and human nature shapes our ethics. Exploring these challenges may entail a far more radical transformation than we realise. Engaging with climate change – as Naomi Klein suggests – could change everything. Yes, it asks us to face our deepest anxieties and unfathomable thoughts but offers to transform us – and our view of "reality" – in the process.

Perhaps this is already happening. We worry that we are not wired to think about climate change but perhaps at the same time there is a change going on inside us, despite ourselves. Perhaps our wiring, itself, is changing. We know about the plasticity of the human brain, but what could have more potential plasticity than the human mind? We may be looking at a very uncertain future but has life ever been so exciting as it is in this 21st century? Science may have given us the means to destroy ourselves but never has the Earth it discloses looked so extraordinary and magical.

Are we being re-wired?

For example we are beginning to feel and see the bigger picture, aesthetically and scientifically. In 1968 who was not moved when we first caught sight of Earth from space in that epoch-changing photo of "Earthrise" from Apollo 8 as it circled the moon?

And in the early 1970s down here on Earth James Lovelock came up with the *Gaia* intuition – the sense of the whole Earth as a living system. What was initially a hypothesis eventually became a theory and was responsible for helping to integrate the earth sciences. If the Earth is the new symbol of transformation and integration, then the question today is whether the human sciences – and particularly psychology – can also become an integral part of "the Earth Sciences".

Cosmology is opening up the universe in extraordinary ways. But also at a subatomic level "matter" itself is looking stranger and more mysterious than ever. There is a growing sense that it has agency – a life of its own – independent of us. The traditional solid dualities are dissolving. What used to be "dead matter" is more alive than we realise and the distinction between organic and inorganic – animate and inanimate – is no longer so sustainable. This may be a new vitalism, experienced as much inside, as outside ourselves. Perhaps what is changing is less the world around us as the lens of the human mind through which we perceive it.

Other contraries are breaking down. The opposition between the "human" and the "non-human" is being questioned. Human nature is no longer so distinct from the natural forces out of which it evolved. To be part of a universal continuum takes us back in a way to the pre-modern teleology of the Great Chain of Being, except that the new chain is not a static structure but a dynamic one – a changing continuity. It evolves in time and doesn't need a mythic creator god.

Along with this there is also a new feeling about the simple fact of existence. There is a new interest in ontology – the fact of our being. Our future may be in doubt but we may come to feel more alive in the present than we ever have. Nor are life and death so much the contraries we in the modern world have made them. Death need no longer be the fearful mystery it has been. More mysterious and magical is life itself – how we come to be here in the first place.

These changes are also mirrored in the creative arts. Extraordinary are the infinite knowledge and interconnections that the world wide web reveals but more innovative is the aesthetic and integrative potential of the human imagination, whether in science, music, the visual arts, theatre and dance, or creative writing. Poetry and narrative literature are as alive as ever but there is a new romanticism to be found in writing on nature, a romanticism which explores how nature and culture are not separate but essentially intertwined. An example is Jay Griffiths' remarkable *Wild: an Elemental Journey* (2008), a book which redefines and re-enchants the human relationship to nature and the wild. Griffiths put her boots on and went to live in such wild places as the Amazon, the Arctic, and outer Mongolia only to find that "wildness" is actually "home" to the humans and other species which live there, a protective, even "kind" place, not the alien, frightening or uncanny wild which modern European Romanticism often made it.

What I am trying to suggest is that our experience of ourselves – our "human nature" and the human mind – is changing and this may be as important – if not more important to us – as the fact of climate change. And if this is so, how are our human sciences – individually and collectively – responding, particularly for us, psychology and psychotherapy? The great nineteenth century Tibetan scholar, Jamgon Kongtrul, proponent of the *Ri-me* – non-sectarian – movement, wrote, reflecting the great and essential insight of Buddhism:

> Just realising the meaning of mind
> encompasses all understanding.

In Jamgon Kongtrul's Buddhist analysis this is not just the human mind but the universe itself – and everything in it – as mind. This is a view obscured to our modern scientific culture. We limit consciousness to ourselves only but are beginning to realise how short-sighted this is. The human mind is an extraordinary phenomenon but it evolved and emerged from something larger than itself.

Psychoanalytic practice

> The new discourse is that of the philosopher
> who thinks from Freud – that is after, with,
> and against him.
> **Paul Ricoeur**

The two great Western figures who initially explored

human psychology through subjective, as well as analytic, experience were William James and Sigmund Freud. While James brought his "radical empiricism" to bear on our experience of consciousness he remained a philosopher. Freud wanted to be a philosopher but remained a physician – of the mind – and teacher, though – in the famous phrase of W.H. Auden's "In Memoriam" – he became "a whole climate of opinion". Freud created a school and, in doing so, devised a practice which students of his art could learn – and develop. The relationship between practice and theory is an interesting one but I have always thought that practice precedes theory. Though theory can help practice, it cannot determine it.

Freud introduced a form of practice without which such innovations as the interpretation of dreams and analysis of the unconscious would have been far less effective. This was the mode of thinking known to us as "free association". As we know the traditional "basic rule" in psychoanalysis – the "talking cure" – is that the patient should report his thoughts without reservation and should make no attempt to concentrate, on the assumption that nothing he says is without significance and that his associations will lead to meaning and insight, insofar as resistance doesn't operate.

Resistance does, of course, operate and traditionally much of the work is about analysing the resistance. Freud thought resistance is lessened by relaxation and often increased by too much concentration. We sometimes forget that, of course, "resistance" can also be interpreted positively – as an assertion of the human spirit.

Interestingly, as Charles Rycroft remarks in his *Critical Dictionary* (1968), "free association" is a mistranslation of the German *freier Einfall* which means "irruption" or "sudden idea" rather than "association" and refers to ideas which present themselves without straining or effort. In this state ideas occur, or happen, to a person from somewhere beyond the rational or logical mind. As Rycroft goes on to explain, this technique enabled Freud to abandon hypnosis and allow the focus to be on the patient who alternates between free association and reflection. An alternative way of thinking about this process is that "the patient oscillates between being the subject and object of his experience, at one moment letting thoughts come, the next moment inspecting them".

Contemplative practice

For me there have always been similarities between

psychotherapeutic practice and contemplative – or meditative – practice, but crucial differences too. Where Freud made the distinction between the relaxed, freely associative subject and the thoughtful, analytical, reflective mind classical Buddhist meditation, for example, also makes a twofold distinction between a calming, tranquil state and the special insight that comes with analytical examination.

In Sanskrit these are known as *shamata* – literally, "dwelling in tranquillity" – and *vipashyana* – insight, clear seeing. *Shamata* is not so much relaxation as a still and alert state where particular attention is initially given to posture and breathing. These are thought to be important because without them insight is limited, even misguided. *Vipashyana* is not so much personal analysis as insight into what Buddhists call "the three marks of existence": impermanence or transience, the truth of suffering, and what they call "no-self", by which they mean egolessness, in an absolute sense. In fact, in the Buddhist understanding, nothing has a self-nature that is fixed, permanent and unchanging – at present most of us unconsciously believe that human nature is a permanent given.

Freud was a scientist but, as a man of culture, he also

belonged to the European Romantic tradition. An important given in that tradition was the cult of the individual which is still a driving factor in our consumerist, capitalist society. From a systemic perspective a person is not so much an individual as an interdependency – whether one is thinking at the level of family, society, or the wider ecology – so a therapeutic practice that is based on interpreting a person's reality from the individual perspective only could be seen as limited, even oppressive. Everyone has individuality but it emerges from an interdependent reality.

A contemplative practice acknowledges this principle and would equate freedom with the realisation of one's interdependency. Early Buddhism encouraged freedom through the individual mind – the *Hinayana,* or narrow tradition of the *arhat,* practiced in isolation – but this became known as the lesser journey and evolved into the greater way – the *Mahayana* or the *Bodhisattva* tradition of enlightened compassion for all beings. The *Hinayana* and the *Mahayana* are not viewed as opposed since compassion for others requires an understanding of oneself, but without the greater view it is thought one cannot realise true freedom and enlightenment.

Knowing oneself

Contemplation involves a paradox which is about using the mind to understand itself – sometimes referred to as "minding mind". In his book, *Luminous Mind* (1997), Kalu Rinpoche, whom the present Dalai Lama compared to Milarepa, the great thirteenth century poet and mystic of Tibet, wrote:

> The basic issue is that it is not possible
> for the mind to know itself because the
> one who searches, the subject, is the mind
> itself, and the object it wants to examine
> is also the mind. There is a paradox here:
> I can look for myself everywhere, search
> the world over, without ever finding myself,
> because I am what I search for.

A paradox is a form of understanding that goes beyond conventional logic or reason and therefore cannot be grasped by conceptual thought only. Hence it is more amenable to the contemplative rather than the rational mind.

Tibetan culture had devoted itself for a thousand years to developing the art and science of meditative introspection, building on the profound Buddhist teachings and practices of India and China before them. Freud – both the phenomenological psychologist as well as the natural scientist – didn't have the benefit of East Asian psychological and philosophical understandings we have today and relied on his own intuitive genius and place in Western cultural thought. As a result he was defeated by this paradox, never became the philosopher – the metaphysician or "metapsychologist" – he aspired to be and called his movement "psychoanalysis" – ultimately a contradiction in terms since in the end the mind cannot be analysed, only experienced and lived.

In the last century the two traditions and practices of "Western" and "Eastern" cultures were thought to be very distinctive, even incompatible. Carl Jung's warnings about our difficulties – or unsuitability – in the Western world to engage in East Asian meditational practices are understandable, given our limited knowledge of the philosophy and psychology behind them at the time. But now we know much more, different cultural traditions are seen to be more complementary than we realised. Many people in the West have turned prematurely to contemplative practices and teachings to address personal difficulties when they would be better starting with some form of psychotherapy which would help them first to establish some personal stability. As has been said, you need to have a self before you can think about no-self. But at the same time people genuinely turn to non-Western contemplative practices because they are thought to address existential and metaphysical issues which our modern culture – and psychotherapy – neglects.

The Secret of the Golden Flower

A contemplative practice will be experienced differently by everybody and grow out of a person's unique disposition and life circumstances. But there are some general understandings and guidelines within the perennial, or ageless, wisdom that have come down to us from all cultural traditions. Take *The Secret of the Golden Flower*, for instance, that *Classic Chinese Book of Life* which Jung and Richard Wilhelm – its original German translator – made known to us as early as 1932. Thomas Cleary published a new and more complete translation from the Chinese in 1991 along with notes and commentaries informed by his extensive knowledge of Taoist and Chan/Zen literature and practices. His edition brings a clarity and depth of understanding that was lacking in the 1932 edition.

As Cleary explains in his introduction, *The Secret of the Golden Flower* is a lay manual of Buddhist and Taoist methods for clarifying the mind. Written some two hundred years ago, it draws upon ancient spiritual Chinese classics and describes a natural way to mental freedom practiced for many centuries. The golden flower symbolizes the quintessence of Buddhist and Taoist paths: "Gold stands for light, the light of the mind itself; the flower represents the blossoming, or opening up, of the light of the mind. Thus the expression is emblematic of the basic awakening of the real self and its hidden potential".

Central to this realisation or awakening of the self is the conscious recognition of the original spirit – the true self – as it is in its spontaneous natural state, independent of environmental conditioning. In the text this original spirit is also called the celestial – or natural – mind, a subtler and more direct mode of awareness than thought or imagination – an invitation, perhaps, to step outside our ideological boxes. Cleary describes the experience of the blossoming of the golden flower as likened to light in the sky, "a sky of awareness vaster than images, thoughts and feelings, an unimpeded space containing everything without being filled. Thus it opens up an avenue to an endless source of intuition, creativity, and inspiration. Once this power of mental awakening has been developed, it can be renewed and deepened without limit".

The Secret of the Golden Flower is a poetic manual containing many helpful meditation techniques but its central method goes beyond techniques, right to the root source of awareness. The core of this method Cleary translates as "Turning the Light Around". It is difficult to describe this in a few words but what is implied is that by turning in towards the light within yourself you become aware that it is not separate, or distinct, from the light within everything else, "outside" you. As the text puts it:

> The light is neither inside nor outside the
> self. Mountains, rivers, sun, moon, and
> the whole earth are all this light, so it is
> not only in the self. All the operations,
> intelligence , knowledge, and wisdom are
> also this light, so it is not outside the self.
> The light of heaven and earth fills the
> universe: the light of one individual also
> naturally extends through the heavens and
> covers the earth. Therefore once you turn
> the light around, everything in the world is
> turned around. (III, 10)

Radical Hope

In this essay I have been trying to say that while, at best, the near future looks very uncertain and our chances of keeping the average global temperature below four degrees – not to mention two – are slim, at the same time we may be experiencing an important awakening within ourselves – psychologically, socially and spiritually. This may come too late to ensure our survival on an Earth currently experiencing a sixth mass extinction but we may be enabled to face it without denial and without giving in to despair. When Naomi Klein declares *This Changes Everything* she also implies "*This*" includes a change within ourselves – more profound than she perhaps realises.

Radical Hope: Ethics in the Face of Cultural Devastation (2008), the title of the philosophical psychoanalyst, Jonathan Lear's book – which Paul (Hoggett), the Chair of the CPA, first drew to our attention and which we discussed at the CPA day in Bristol in April, 2015 – examines the paradox of a hopeless hope. This is a hope beyond conventional hope but also beyond despair – Lear writes of "courage and hope" in contrast to "mere optimism". He describes the loss of the way of life of the indigenous North American Crow nation when the buffalo were wiped out in the nineteenth century and

47

they no longer could do battle with the Sioux, their common enemy. As Plenty Coups, the chief of the Crow, lamented, "when the buffalo went away the hearts of my people fell to the ground and they could not lift them up again. After this nothing happened". But this "nothing" proved anything but an empty nothing for out of it the Crow were able to find a new way of life.

In *Radical Hope* Lear describes how with the loss of their culture the Crow found themselves "reasoning at the abyss" – they faced a "radical discontinuity" with their past which involved "a disruption in the sense of being", like "a rip in the fabric of one's self". Plenty Coups did not give in to despair but accepted the demise of his culture with courage and a faith that something would emerge out of the abyss.

Accordingly at the Tomb of the Unknown Soldier he laid down his "coup stick" – the emblem of his warrior culture – acknowledging that the traditional ways of the Crow had to be laid to rest before a new life could begin to be imagined. What made his hope "radical" was that it was accompanied by a faith in a future goodness. In Lear's words: "Radical hope anticipates a good for which those who have this hope as yet lack the appropriate concepts with which to understand it". This is what makes Lear's book a study in ethics.

Everything and Nothing

> The actual discipline or practice of the
> Bodhisattva is to regard whatever occurs as
> a phantom (dream). Nothing ever happens.
> But because nothing happens, everything
> happens ... that "nothing happening" is the
> experience of openness.
>
> **Chogyam Trungpa, *Training the Mind***

The parallels with the challenge to our own culture in a time of climate change are very clear. The big difference is when nothing "happened" to the Crow, at least they had the opportunity of an actual future – a new sense of being could emerge, the rip in their fabric of the self could be addressed. Our "nothing" on the contrary, implies the collapse of everything. The ethical challenge we now face is an absolute, not a relative one – how to conceive of a "good life" – and a benign universe – when there is the possibility of no future at all. The questions multiply as we reason at our own abyss: how do we think beyond death? How is it possible to live ethically in the face of our own demise? What meaning can we give it? How must it change our view of ourselves? Where do we find the courage, faith and understanding we now need?

I have suggested one way of trying to answer this last question. For the Crow it was not about simply exchanging their traditional way of life for our modern one, so – for us – it is not about turning away from our own culture but seeing how we might begin to learn from others – learning ways that we could begin to integrate with our own. There is an intriguing question that runs through all the ancient Indian *Upanishads*, those sacred writings that are thousands of years old:

> What is that by knowing
> which all things are known?

The answer in the *Upanishads* is: knowledge of the true or original self – incidentally a knowledge which enables a contemporary American exponent of the perennial philosophy like Ken Wilber for instance, to write books with such titles as *A Brief History of Everything* (1996) and *A Theory of Everything* (2001). Everything and Nothing are not opposites. Everything comes from Nothing. The question is: do we have the courage to face our Nothing? As for an "ethics in the face of cultural devastation" we are badly in need of this. The Tibetans have a tradition of seven-point mind training they have used for centuries. It is called *Lojong* and consists of 59 pithy slogans which are a means to awaken the kindness, gentleness, and compassion which are core to the training. Central to the actual practice is *bodhicitta* or "awakened mind".

There are two levels of bodhicitta – relative and ultimate. Relative is about attaining liberation through compassion for all beings and practicing meditation to achieve this, while ultimate bodhicitta is viewed as the vision of the true nature of everything – *shunyata.* Since we are currently facing the ultimate challenge, this teaching could not be more timely. A number of commentaries have been published but the ones I have found helpful – in addition to the original modern English translation by Chogyam Trungpa, *Training the Mind* (1993, 2003) – are Pema Chodron, *Start Where You Are: How to Accept Yourself and Others* (2005), B. Alan Wallace, *The Seven-Point Mind Training: A Tibetan Method for Cultivating Mind and Heart* (2013) and the classic commentary by Jamgon Kongtrul – *The Great Path of Awakening: The Classic Guide to Lojong,* translated by Ken McLeod (1987, 2018).

Although I originally began by making the case for doing nothing this is not a passive, but an active, mindful and meaningful nothing. The need to be active has never been more urgent but it is also a time for pausing and reviewing all our values – about who and what we essentially are. In classical China this was known as *Stopping and Seeing*. Climate change may be our ultimate challenge but it is also an opportunity. It is scary to think about what the future may hold, but it may well also bring an awakening.

Paradoxically, there is something strengthening about contemplating the worst that could happen. Only when we go beyond the hope of survival on the one hand and despair at the thought of catastrophe on the other can we really be empowered. In these very challenging times one way of avoiding despair at the difficulty of the task is to remember the third of the Seven Points of Mind Training:

> The Transformation of Adversity into the
> Path of Awakening – when misfortune fills
> the world and its inhabitants, make adversity
> the path of awakening.

November, 2015

Awakening:
Further thoughts on Radical Hope

When misfortune fills the world and its
inhabitants, make adversity the path of
awakening.

Jamgon Kongtrul,
The Great Path of Awakening
(Tr. by Ken McLeod)

This paper is a follow-up to one I originally posted, entitled "Everything and Nothing", on the old Climate Psychology Alliance (CPA) website in June 2015, but which was included in the new website in November of that year. The paper was partly a response to the CPA day on Radical Hope held in Bristol in April and an attempt to understand what is meant by "radical hope", as distinct from simple optimism. I also tried to explore how we might return to some of the perennial, or ultimate, values we have lost sight of in these very uncertain times.

In "Everything and Nothing" I referred to the scientific consensus that, as many who read this know, unless we curb our carbon emissions dramatically and quickly, we are heading towards an average temperature rise of four degrees this century, with all the implications for our "civilised" way of life and for all life on Earth. The first step in any kind of "awakening" must be awareness of this threat.

Yet awareness of climate change, and the threat of extinction that comes with it, seems impossible for many to contemplate. It is perhaps not so surprising that denial and business-as-usual is the common response. While Greens have been aware of the ecological implications of our consumer culture – and have been warning about it – for some fifty years the CPA has recently formed to ask why, when disaster now looms more and more clearly, too many people continue to ignore it. Facing the reality about climate change today, as affiliates to the CPA realise, can be shocking and traumatising. No wonder we are drawn to despair. I was thinking about this after seeing one of the co-founders of CPA, Judith Anderson's, recent response to yet another article she was posting on the CPA googlegroup about the ever growing signs – this time the unprecedented event of hundreds of icebergs breaking off the Greenland peninsula and floating out into the North Atlantic. Judith's brief and understandable remark accompanying the link was: "I expect some of you have read this report. Weep".

Judith's comment also put me in mind of George Monbiot's impassioned and informed columns in the Guardian. I used to wonder how he managed to maintain his motivation as he fumed week after week at our relative political inertia in the face of mounting evidence of ecological degradation. When would he also simply break down and weep? I asked myself. Did he ever feel like giving up?

But it's crucial we don't just despair. Nor do we have to. Why George Monbiot and many others don't give up is a good question, and one that we might do well to think more about. It raises for me an issue for the CPA. What do we do after we acknowledge our feelings of despair and hopelessness? I am not sure whether a purely therapeutic culture has an answer to this. Therapy, psychoanalytic or otherwise, will help and encourage us to face difficult feelings but I wonder whether "therapy" itself is a sufficient response to the climate emergency. It may be a start but, in its anthropocentrism, is it still too entangled in a modern Western culture responsible for the emergency in the first place?

Perplexity

> For manifestly you have long been aware of what you mean when you use the expression 'being'; we, however, who used to think we have understood it have become perplexed.
> **Plato, translated by Martin Heidegger in *Being and Time***

We live in a time of great perplexity. There are the current local questions of why the U.K. voted to leave the European Community and the U.S. elected a president who seems temperamentally and intellectually unsuitable for the office. But more than this are the wider issues that perplex us: why, when we have the technology to feed the world, so many millions are starving and dying; why, when we devote so much intellectual energy to the science of economics there is a huge and increasing gap between the rich and the poor, within and between nations; why there is so much hate and anger in the world; why there are terrorist groups who kill themselves and others against all ethical wisdom; and why, of course, when we know our carbon economy is set to doom all life on Earth, we are doing too little about it.

Perplexity in itself is not a reason for despair. On the contrary there are those who think it is our natural condition. After all, we really don't know what the universe is for. Or what we are doing here in it. It was Martin Heidegger's view that the meaning of our being involves the questioning of it. In other words, who we are is an issue for us. In a recent book, *A Case for Irony (The Tanner Lectures on Human Values)* (2014), the philosopher and psychoanalyst, Jonathan Lear, who also wrote *Radical Hope,* argued for the return of irony, not in the conventional sense of irony as clever or satirical thinking, but irony as real perplexity. He cited Socrates as a prime exemplar. When Socrates is interpreted as a dissembler and gadfly by his interlocutors in Plato's dialogues, they assume that he knows the answers to his own persistent questions when, in truth, he doesn't. Socrates is genuinely perplexed but believes this to be a more honest basis for an ethical, good, or excellent life, even worth taking the poison for! Only in perplexity can one discover true knowledge, attainable by first recognising our own ignorance and delusion.

There are degrees of knowledge and perplexity, of course, as there are certainty and uncertainty. Just before he died E.F.Schumacher, famous for *Small is Beautiful: A Study of Economics as if People Mattered* (1973) handed the manuscript of his last book, *Guide for the Perplexed* (1977) to his daughter, telling her that it contained the core of wisdom that his life had been leading up to. In the opening chapter "On Philosophical Maps" he pointed out that, by looking for certain knowledge we may miss out on what may be the subtlest, most important and most rewarding things in life and he quoted St Thomas Aquinas, following Aristotle, that "the slenderest knowledge that may be obtained of the highest things is more desirable than the most certain knowledge of lesser things." "Slender" knowledge indicates uncertainty and Schumacher comments: "Maybe it is not necessarily so that the higher things cannot be known with the same degree of certainty as the lesser things can be known, in which case it would be a very great loss indeed if knowledge were limited to things beyond the possibility of doubt."

It is important that we leave room for uncertainty when

predicting, as science does, the material consequences of our fossil fuel economy, if only to allow ourselves to think about climate change in more than just scientific terms. To contemplate its meaning and significance for us in a philosophical and existential sense may be as important as weighing up the practical consequences. Should the CPA be thinking about this? Perhaps there are more crucial things than merely our survival. Perhaps if we gave thought to these we might be more likely to survive, along with the rest of life.

Contemplating climate change

> Nothing compares to making the affliction itself
> into medicine.
> ***The Secret of the Golden Flower***
> (Tr. by Thomas Cleary)

The challenge of climate change may be the most difficult we face, given the threat to our existence, but its contemplation, beyond the question of our survival, may also lead to new and transformed understandings about ourselves and the universe we live in. As I have mentioned before, modern Western science may have provided us with the means to destroy ourselves along with all life on the Planet but never has the Earth it discloses looked more mysterious and magical. To think how we might also be a part of the mystery and magic could counter-balance the despair. The European Enlightenment tradition developed the simple belief that all knowledge might be accumulated in one hubristic encyclopaedic venture – a circle of knowledge – that contained all there was to know. And this remains a conscious or unconscious belief of many orthodox scientists, despite the twentieth century revolutions of relativity and quantum mechanics.

Science is, however, undergoing a new revolution, transforming itself from its adherence to the dogmatic assumptions of materialist and secular ideology and turning to an appreciation of the lifeworld within everything – from the endless reaches of subatomic matter to the infinite spaces of the cosmos, as well as to the immaterial dimension in the human mind and its place on the life spectrum. In fact the science of mind may be our key to bridging the imagined gap between the material and the immaterial worlds, and core to any awakening in this century.

This may also be the heart of an integral consciousness which Schumacher writes about and which can help "guide" us through our perplexities. It is at the centre of any perennial philosophy. It is the "unity consciousness" that Ken Wilber expounds in one of his most popular and readable books, *No Boundary* (1980) written as a follow-up to his first, more difficult *The Spectrum of Consciousness* (1979). *No Boundary,* subtitled *Eastern and Western Approaches to Personal Growth,* is a slim but comprehensive account and map of the world's psychologies and therapies, from psychoanalysis to Zen, existentialism to Tantra. It may be an important text for any psychological approach to climate science.

Integral consciousness

The spirit of integrative thinking applies to all our human endeavours. It is helpful to explore how the different psychological and therapeutic approaches relate to each other but more important is the integration of everything. No one discipline alone can tell us how to face climate change, the new meta-context for all our thinking. We all need, in the wise words of the American nun, Pema Chodron, to "start where we are" but we don't need to stay there. What was heartening about last year's leadership conference in London, organised by the CPA committee, was the way it brought people together from different fields in a common dialogue. This has been happening elsewhere, of course, for some time but what was significant in this event was that the initiative was taken by the Psychology Alliance, signalling that there needs to be a dimension of psychological understanding in the overall movement. Interestingly, people from other fields seem to be much more open to a psychological perspective than psychological professionals sometimes are to ecological perspectives.

The value of an integrative and dialogic approach is that everyone learns from each other, both in how you learn what others are doing in their own spheres but what you also learn about your own speciality by trying to communicate it to people outside. There is a strong possibility that individual disciplines, psychology for instance, may be transformed in the process.

This suggests that integrative thinking is not only about inter-disciplinary initiatives. The boundaries between different subjects may be radically changed but this may lead in turn to intra-disciplinary transformations as well as inter-disciplinary ones. This would also facilitate the creation of new and shared concepts, including the language used to express them. Psychologists and psychotherapists tend to be more conservative in this respect so it may be more challenging for us, but exciting for those who take the risk. The integrative spirit also pervades the thinking behind the idea of a "progressive alliance" today that promises to transform political thinking in the future.

The One and the Many

Integrative thinking is not just about seeing the pattern within our relationships with each other and with the subject areas that individually preoccupy us, but also about understanding what the anthropologist, Gregory Bateson, called "the pattern that connects" within all things. The philosopher, Baruch Spinoza, who was a contemporary of Renee Descartes, was famous for his description of the universe as a single unity. In Spinoza's seventeenth century conceptualisation, God and nature are one "substance",as against Descartes' assertion of the dichotomy of mind and matter which our modern scientific culture is built upon. Spinoza was accused of being a pantheist and atheist and excommunicated but, like the ancient Neo-Platonists, he could be seen as following Plotinus' notion of the One and the Many – the uni-verse as One, or as the Buddhists say "One Taste" and the Many as the infinite emanations of the One, "The Ten Thousand Things" according to the Chinese, which come from the One.

This touches on the core of poetic truth. When W.B.Yeats famously wrote in his 1920 poem, "The Second Coming":

> Things fall apart: the centre cannot hold
> mere anarchy is loosed upon the world

and T.S. Eliot in "The Waste Land" asked and asserted around the same time:

> What are the roots that clutch, what branches grow
> Out of this stony rubbish?
> ...A heap of broken images

they encapsulated the sense of fragmentation and chaos that characterise our modern age. William Blake, however, had also expressed the life-enhancing potential of the poetic spirit in his "Auguries of Innocence" only a little more than a hundred years before:

> To see a World in a Grain of Sand
> And a Heaven in a Wild Flower,
> Hold Infinity in the palm of your hand
> And Eternity in an hour

Beyond poetic truth

Poetic truth is no observer of conventional boundaries. It moves, as the philosopher, Alexandre Koyre, put it in the title of his classic book – which Blake would doubtless have approved of – *From the Closed World to the Infinite Universe* (1957). It takes us beyond itself. Ken Wilber's notion of *No Boundary* is a re-description of the Buddhist concept of "emptiness", the experience of mind beyond conceptual or imaginative thinking.

"Emptiness" doesn't mean literally no boundary. It means that, while in a relative world there will always be boundaries, in an absolute sense the universe is a seamless unity without boundaries, An awareness of absolute emptiness doesn't simply efface boundaries, it allows us to keep redrawing them and bringing more clarity and vividness into our understanding of ourselves and the world around us. The shortest, perhaps most famous of Buddhist wisdom sutras – *The Heart Sutra* – reminds us that form, or structure, and emptiness go together. You cannot have one without the other. They are always re-defining each other.

We have lost touch with the sense of emptiness – the essential reality of absolute space, inner as well as outer – that helps us to redraw the boundaries. A boundary is not a fixed thing but a moving process. Nor is it just something that separates us, but the line that joins, relates and integrates. Like any membrane, though, it needs to breathe. It is our essential source of inspiration. We need to keep moving with it. And where best to start than with our own minds? In the psychological assessment of people in my work I used to draw encouragement from Andrew (Samuel)'s enlightened notions of the "political" and "plural psyche", as extending what we thought of as "psychological". His books prompted me to think also of the scientific, economic, social and religious, or spiritual, psyche? In the end mind goes beyond all boundaries.

Who, or what, are we?

> When an extreme is reached, there is a
> reversion.
> ***The Secret of the Golden Flower***
> (Tr. by Thomas Cleary)

What I am suggesting is that just as we face an unprecedented planetary emergency, so it is also an opportunity to redefine ourselves and ask who we essentially are. Andrew Simms, fellow of the new economics foundation, gave the first

Coleridge lecture of the New Weather Institute in Bristol last year (2015), which was published with the title: *We are more than this.* In it he highlighted how any "new economics" hinges on the meaning we give to human nature. He suggested that neo-liberal economics is predicated on three assumptions about our "dark" personality traits: "Machiavellianism (tendencies to deceit), narcissism (over-inflated sense of self-worth) and psychopathy (lack of guilt and remorse)."Simms goes on to ask whether humanity really does "smell this bad" and to ask whether our notion of "economic man" is ready to be "removed from the centre of our theoretical solar system, much as the Earth once had to be replaced by the Sun to correct a similar mistaken belief." This is a very interesting thought.

Could it be that our modern human-centred psychology is also akin to a Ptolemaic system that patched up a solar system with ever more complicated epicycles to prove deludedly that the Sun does go round the Earth? It was not until a thousand years later Johannes Kepler, following Copernicus and Galileo, emerged to put the Sun back in the centre and suggest that we were elliptically, not centrally, related to it – and the rest of the universe. It could be said that Kepler's de-centering of the Earth let light back into our thinking and prepared the way for Newton and the European Enlightenment? Perhaps we are ready for a new psychological enlightenment. Perhaps we are about to learn that we are here for the Earth, not that the Earth is here for us. Perhaps we need a Declaration of Human Responsibilities as well as Human Rights. Is it time we let go of our fixed, hard-wired view of "human nature" and realise we are now waking up to a more liberated understanding of ourselves? In the far-east there has always been the notion of an original *buddha* – or awakened – *nature* beyond the idea of human nature. This is our essential nature, not separate from human nature but contextual to it.

At the same time a new global balance may be in sight between the world-views of East and West. While the philosophical and psychological essence of *buddha dharma* has been revered and developed in Tibet over the last thousand years, the West has evolved a social, political, and economic awareness – though, in its purely capitalist drive, lacking a sufficiently ethical dimension. Integrating the insights of the inner, psychological world of the East with the social and political understandings of the West would help us bridge the gap between the "two cultures" – within and between different cultures – which has bedevilled our history.

Adaequatio

The beauties of the highest heavens and the
marvels of the sublimest realms are all within
the heart: this is where the perfectly open and
aware spirit concentrates. Confucians call it
the open center, Buddhists call it the pedestal
of awareness, Taoists call it the ancestral
Earth, the yellow court, the mysterious pass,
the primal opening.

The Secret of the Golden Flower
(Tr. by Thomas Cleary)

To effect this integration requires both traditions to acknowledge their limitations as well as their achievements. In the East there has been suppression of scientific and political evolution while the Western philosophical and psychological disciplines have proscribed a practice that promises to take them beyond scientific and analytic thought. In his *Guide for the Perplexed* Ernst Schumacher devotes two chapters to the principle of "'adequacy" which addresses the question of how we are enabled to know anything about the world around us. Plotinus said "Knowing demands the organ fitted to the object." In other words nothing can be known without there being an appropriate "instrument" in the makeup of the knower. As Schumacher writes: "This is the Great Truth of *adaequatio* (adequateness), which defines knowledge as *adaequatio rei et intellectus:* the understanding of the knower must be *adequate* to the thing to be known."

Plotinus famously said in his essay on "Beauty": "Never did eye see the sun unless it had first become sunlike, and never can the soul have vision of the First Beauty unless itself be beautiful." This is expressed in Vedantic thought as "That Art Thou", illustrated and expounded by Aldous Huxley in the first chapter of his landmark anthology and study, *The Perennial Philosophy,* first published in 1944. It is the principle that we are composed of the very world we like to think we are objectively examining. In order to really know it, should we not also examine ourselves as an expression of that (objective) world that appears so perplexing to us?

In order to be "adequate" requires us to develop a practice that goes beyond analytic thinking. Freud and the psychoanalytic tradition have shown us how to explore the personal mind and its passions but has stopped short of an experience of mind that goes beyond the personal. Jung, of course, went much further, as did other transpersonal therapists, and schools of systemic therapy have developed the reality of family and "stranger-group" processes, demonstrating the connections between inter-personal and intra-personal processes.

But whereas the practice of contemplative "science" has historically been regarded – and persecuted – as heretical in the West and confined to its poetic and literary traditions, in the East its mystics have been celebrated and revered. The challenge today is how to integrate the scientific insights of the inner world of the East with the material scientific and political knowledge of Europe and the modern West. Isn't this what a global consciousness should aim for, rather than simply establish an economic, trading globalisation? It's what the ancient Silk Road made possible, wisdom accompanying trade. Perhaps the spirit of the Silk Road has now begun to extend globally into Europe, the Americas, and beyond.

The value of integrative practice

An integrative practice encourages us to look beyond our own disciplines and see ourselves from other perspectives. Andrew Simms, suggests, for instance, how, from an alternative view of economics, we might also think differently about psychology. In a well-known parable Buddhism tells how we are all like blind people describing the nature of an elephant by assuming it is to be identified with the single anatomical part each can touch and feel. The shape of the whole elephant only becomes evident when we talk to each other and are able to form a composite or integrated picture.

I have been reading Pankaj Mishra's recent book, *Age of Anger* (2017) about the "great waves of paranoid hatreds that seem inescapable in our close-knit world". It strikes me that he provides a good example of a fresh perspective from the East of the elephant of the European and Western mind. He would perhaps approve of this comparison because, in addition to his extensive knowledge of Western culture, he has also written a personal account of his own experience of Buddhism, *An End to Suffering* (2004). His writings provide original insights into the Western mind from an Asian perspective, the outside as it were, while at the same time being more "inside" it than many of us are. For me he impressively reframes European history and thought and is an example of integrative thinking on a global scale.

Entering into dialogue with others can be difficult and challenging because of the different technical or idiosyncratic languages everyone uses. It's enjoyable and rewarding, of course, to learn new languages, but it's also important to look for a common language or currency. Perhaps this would be helped if we were to focus on the common values that unite, as well as the different languages that differentiate us. The core value spheres are ethics, science, and aesthetics – or art – known classically as the Good, the True, and the Beautiful – or even sublime.

These value spheres apply to all our endeavours and it is important to think of them as a unity. Ethics has to be wise and aesthetic to be authentic or it becomes a mindless and unattractive morality. Science, whether natural or human, likewise should be ethical and sensitive to itself as also an art form to be true science or it becomes an instrumental and technocratic scientism. Art should also take account of the Good and the True to go beyond itself, or it can become purely subjective and self-referential. These are values we can measure all our different activities and thinking by.

Awakening to a timeless perspective

> We don't have to change to awaken, we have
> only to awaken to change.
> **Mark Epstein, *Going On Being***

Finally I want to argue for retaining a wider sense of perspective amidst all the bad news now coming our way. I am always amazed at the equanimity and humour of the Dalai Lama and his fellow lamas around the world, maintained despite the killing of hundreds of thousands of their people and the destruction of countless Tibetan temples by the Chinese in the last century. They seem to know how to wear their suffering lightly. Are they aware of something we have lost sight of? Although the first great truth Gautama Buddha taught was the existence of suffering, this was followed by three other great truths which teach how to understand and overcome suffering. In the words of the *Anguttara-Nikaya:* "He who recognises the existence of suffering, it's cause, it's remedy, and its cessation, has fathomed the four noble truths. He will walk in the right path."

One of the causes of suffering is ignorance and the point of the Buddhist story of The Blind Men and the Elephant is to deepen our perspective on the world by opening our eyes to the views of others. Climate change and ecological depredation are one immediate challenge but they are also our greatest opportunity. Out of the seeming chaos all around us a new and exciting order may be emerging.

Yes, we need to see our specialised areas of knowledge and experience in a more unified and integrated way. But do we not also need to go beyond our purely human perspective, perhaps to reflect on Aquinas' "slenderest knowledge of the highest things" or to see everything, in Spinoza's phrase, *sub specie aeternitatis,* in the light of eternity?

One day the cosmos will continue, of course, without us. The Earth is a tiny dot, a speck in an infinite universe, as our cosmologists have demonstrated. But for now what a dot, what a speck! where life and mind, including *homo sapiens,* with all his imperfections, has emerged and evolved. The French mathematician and philosopher, Blaise Pascal – who was terrified by the vastness of space – wrote that while human beings may be, "like reeds, the weakest thing in nature, they are thinking reeds". He also reminded us we have hearts, and that "the heart has its reasons which reason knows nothing of".

The great metaphysicians testify that the sheer fact of life – of Being, of "Isness" – is supreme. The death, or non-being, we so much fear, is not the opposite of life but included in it. In his famous essay, "*To philosophise Is to learn how to die*", Montaigne, who thought we shouldn't be afraid of dying, reminded us death was a part of the order of the universe, an integral part of the life of the world. In other words death is not a thing in itself – neither our individual nor collective death. Nor does it have to have dominion over us.

Moreover, while Life includes death, it itself is indestructible, as, incredibly, are we. We may feel like a drop in the ocean, but the indestructible ocean is in us, or, as the title of the Dalai Lama's book about modern science describes it, *The Universe* (is) *in a Single Atom* (2007). Is it not time to realise our identity with everything around us? The unity of the great chain of Life – the One and the Ten Thousand Things – is the essential truth we need to re-awaken to, for it promises to sustain us through all our daily fears, anxieties, and terrors.

May 2017

Where has Truth Gone?

Review of books by Naomi Klein, Pankaj Mishra and Ken Wilber

No is Not Enough: Defeating the New Shock Politics
by Naomi Klein
ALLEN LANE: 2017, 273 PP

Age of Anger: A History of the Present
by Pankaj Mishra
ALLEN LANE: 2017, 406 PP

Trump and a Post-Truth World
by Ken Wilber
SHAMBHALA: 2017, 145 PP

Two days after the Brexit referendum I found myself at a conference in Bristol. The focus of the conference was quite wide-ranging – on cultural approaches to current world problems – but you can imagine where our minds and feelings were focused. The atmosphere and sense of shock that pervaded the weekend was understandable, as was the anger and confusion, but what I wasn't prepared for was the degree of contempt, hostility and condescension of the mainly Southern and educated members towards the "stupid" and "ignorant" people in the country who voted leave. I voted to remain but, coming from a region in the North where the leave vote was quite high, I was shocked at the level of antagonism that was being expressed in the conference. Feeling quite angry myself, I pointed out we live in a democracy and that many of the leave voters will have experienced a steady decline in their living standards for a number of years which they felt neither the rich elite of Southern England, nor the bureaucrats of Brussels had done anything about. If similar dynamics held sway in the US, then the stage, it seems, was set for the election of Trump.

The shock has continued to reverberate and we are faced with a conservative government, reeling from divisions and further setbacks affecting their Brexit negotiations, and a

Trump administration that threatens the worst for the planet. There is of course a daily avalanche of comment in the UK on Brexit and across the world on Trump but the books reviewed here are three immediate responses by otherwise scholarly and thoughtful authors who also take the long cultural view. Perhaps the speed of publication speaks for the depth of anxiety as well as the hope of possibility they feel. All demonstrate the need to go beyond shock, anger and bewilderment and to think clearly about what we can learn from current developments. Naomi Klein builds on her climate change perspective and suggests how the left might open itself to a new sense of vision that offers a real alternative to the doomed ideology of neoliberalism. Pankaj Mishra points to the European historical roots of the anger and *ressentiment* – including the global terrorist phenomena – that characterise the end of the twentieth and early twenty-first century, while Ken Wilber, drawing as he does on perennial traditions throughout world history, offers the widest possible cultural analysis of our post-truth age.

Our own shadow

All three books also point to the importance of recognising our own collective shadow in recent events if we are to try to understand them. This is crucial to knowing the truth about ourselves. Climate change and mass extinction face us with the prospect of our own imminent demise. In the classic psychological responses to a terminal condition – our "end times" – shock is an initial stage, followed, or accompanied, by grief, anger, and depression before some sort of understanding, acceptance, active reparation and radical hope can also emerge. The political reverses of recent times offer us the possibility of addressing all these responses, but do we not also have to take a good, honest look at ourselves? Wilber published two books this year, the one under review here and the other, a major work, *The Religion of Tomorrow: A Vision for the Future of the Great Traditions,* which emphasises the importance of shadow work as a prelude to understanding ourselves.

The term "shadow" was used by Jung, though of course the work of analysing the darker side of one's personality also belongs to Freud before him. Everyone, and every group, carries a shadow and the more we ignore or repress it, the darker and more fearful it seems. In *A Critical Dictionary of Jungian Analysis* (1986) Andrew Samuels, Bani Shorter and Fred Plaut quote Jung's definition of the shadow in 1945: "the thing a person has no wish to be". Hence we project it onto others and events outside. But by facing the truth about ourselves we can learn from it. If we don't, it is likely to burst out and overwhelm us. This is a basic understanding in any form of psychotherapy.

The idea that Trump – the fake president? – mirrors something in us is a difficult thought to concede. With his shameless worship of money and all things shiny and glossy he embodies the worst side of our consumer society. Perhaps his addictions mirror the shadow of our own greed? After all, our press helped to get him elected while our fixation on his worst personal qualities distracts us from addressing the reality of his neoliberal administration, now doing its best, as Naomi Klein illuminates, to deconstruct any ecological initiatives towards a better world.

At the same time our obsessive attention to Trump's negative qualities may be blinding us to the possibility of light in this shadow. Psychoanalytic approaches tend to emphasise the split between light and dark, whereas the truth is simply that you cannot have one without the other. All light casts a shadow. Look into the shadow and you come back to the light. Our liberal "enlightened" leadership has failed us. Trump's shock election has given us the opportunity to reflect on this. Perhaps we should thank him for that at least.

NAOMI KLEIN

Klein acknowledges that *NO IS NOT ENOUGH* is different from her previous books. *NO LOGO, No Space, No Choice, No Jobs,* published in 2000 and *THE SHOCK DOCTRINE, The Rise of Disaster Capitalism* (2007) are lengthy, thoroughly researched but timely and explosive works which each took a number of years to write. By contrast she wrote and published *NO IS NOT ENOUGH, Defeating the New Shock Politics,* this year in a matter of months, though draws on all the work she did in her previous books to explain why Trump is no aberration "but the entirely predictable, indeed cliched outcome of ubiquitous ideas and trends that should have been stopped long ago". And of course she also writes in the perspective of *THIS CHANGES EVERYTHING. Capitalism versus the Climate* (2014) which adds a whole new dimension and power to her arguments.

In her introduction Klein describes a strange feeling, as she watched Trump's rise to power, that behind the "shock politics" were a range of trends that she has documented over the years:

> The rise of Superbrands, the expanding
> powers of private wealth over the

> political system, the global imposition of
> neoliberalism, often using racism and fear
> of the 'other' as a potent tool, the damaging
> impacts of corporate free trade, and the deep
> hold that climate change denial has taken on
> the right side of the political spectrum.

The more she thought about it the more Trump seemed to her like "Frankenstein's monster, sewn together out of the body parts of all of these and many other dangerous trends".

He is a "monster" because behind the "domestic shock doctrine", designed to create maximum confusion and disorientation amongst the public, lies the goal to pursue "all-out war on the public sphere and the public interest" and the establishment of unfettered power and freedom for corporations, a programme "so defiantly unjust and so manifestly corrupt that it can only be pulled off with the assistance of divide-and-conquer racial and sexual politics", as well as "a nonstop spectacle of media distractions" which are being backed up by a massive increase in war spending and "a dramatic escalation of military conflicts on multiple fronts, from Syria to North Korea, alongside presidential musings how 'torture works'".

Corporate takeover

Trump's cabinet speaks for itself: Exxon Mobil for secretary of state, General Dynamics and Boeing to head the Department of Defence, and Goldman Sachs for many of the other jobs. All seem to be focused on what Steve Bannon openly declared was "the deconstruction of the administrative state". Klein calls this "a naked corporate takeover". Of course Trump had his own ambitious money-making reasons for being elected to the top dog position – the presidency of the most powerful state in the world – as the extension of his own personal super brand, "the Trump presidency", but behind his personal ambition is a group of super-rich business men who have dispensed with the whole idea of politics and any ethical values associated with it. As Klein writes in her introduction:

> A near-impenetrable sense of impunity – of
> being above the usual rules and laws – is
> a defining feature of this administration.
> Anyone who presents a threat to that
> impunity is summarily fired... Up to now
> there's been a mask on the corporate state's
> White House proxies: the smiling actor's face
> of Ronald Reagan or the faux cowboy persona
> of George W. Bush..... Now the mask is gone.

And no one is even bothering to pretend
otherwise.

Klein's account of how "Trump won by becoming the ultimate brand" and established "the first family of brands" is shocking itself, as are the "games" at Mar-a-Lago, Trump's own "White House" residence in Florida. He sees the presidency in terms of reality tv and, no politician himself, is more at home in the crude bullying practices of *The Apprentice* and the fake antics of the wrestling profession. As Klein says, "The Trump Show is now broadcasting live from the Oval Office."

Trump is immune to scandal because he doesn't play by political rules. Nor is it possible to see any consistent principled pattern in his unpredictable behaviour and thinking. He seems to recognise no values except those that promote his own personal brand. As long as he remains true to his brand and makes more and more money, he is invulnerable. But that, says Klein, is also his weak point. If the bubble of his brand can be "jammed" and he starts to lose money, he will have been deprived of the value and logic by which he, and his administration, lives.

Resisting the shock tactics

Where do we start? In *No Logo* Klein suggested how "to take aim at the brand bullies". In *No Is Not Enough* she points out any distinction between the Trump brand and the Trump presidency is "a concept the current occupant of the White House cannot begin to comprehend. The presidency is the crowning extension of the Trump brand". Beyond that Trump is a "hollow man". The more we are shocked by his contradictory behaviour and unpredictable mind, and just say No to him, the more we feed into his game. No isn't enough. We have to start by not being shocked, understand the rules he plays by and find an alternative way of responding. We have to develop what Klein calls "a road map of shock resistance".

Klein has learned in reporting from dozens of locations in the midst of crisis that it is possible to find ways of resisting shock tactics. Two crucial things have to happen. First we need a good understanding how shock politics work and whose interests they serve. This is "how we get out of shock quickly and start fighting back."

Second, and just as important "we have to tell a *different* story from the one the shock doctors are peddling, a vision of the world compelling enough to compete head-to-head with theirs." This must be "a values-based vision....one based on coming together across racial, ethnic, religious and gender divides....one based on healing the planet rather than unleashing further destabilising wars and pollution." She adds that most of all that vision needs "to offer those who are hurting – for lack of jobs, lack of health care, lack of peace, lack of hope – a tangibly better life". George Monbiot, the *Guardian* columnist, also wrote – "How do we get out of this mess?" September 17th – about the importance of telling an alternative story to the traditional one of competitive and possessive individualism. Altruism and cooperation are more fundamental to our nature than we recognise. Knowing this is the essential antidote to despair.

The question is how do we go about building Klein's vision? In her introduction she doesn't claim to know what it looks like, but by part 4, "How Things Could Get Better", she offers us a range of ideas with practical examples. Firstly she suggests, when faced with shared trauma, or common threat, there are signs communities can come together in "defiant acts of sanity and maturity". Rebecca Solnit wrote, for instance, of the extraordinary communities that can arise in disaster in her original, even exhilarating book, *A Paradise Built in Hell.*

Secondly, the blitzkrieg strategy of the shock doctrine is actually quite high risk. If it doesn't succeed in demoralising people it could have the opposite effect of uniting them. There is the experience of Argentina in the early 2000s when in the *asambleas barriales* (neighbourhood communities) people assembled to resist the policing and austerity measures of their prime minister, Fernando de la Rua. Similarly when Spain's president, Jose Maria Aznar, tried to bring in firm and reactionary policies following the terrorist bombing of a Madrid commuter train in March 2004 the Spanish people refused to be cowed either by the terrorism or the extreme reaction of the government. Interestingly, fifteen years on, and when the terrorism is more frequent, we might observe there are examples of calmer and more reflective responses to terrorist attacks amongst communities. After the bombing at the Manchester Arena Centre this year the town came together in a spirit of defiant solidarity and community feeling. Similarly in Barcelona people flooded La Rambla the day after the vehicle attack in August. Perhaps fear is now having less hold on people.

Sheer facts and interior realities

Other factors weighing against the neoliberal view are what Klein terms "The Revenge of Reality", the sheer facts of science – whether about climate change or the increasingly obvious truth of mass extinction – and how these realities are influencing the activities of more and more people. With the World Wide Web and information sources like Wikipedia, the average person is so much more knowledgeable – at a time when Trump seems to take pride in his ignorance and twitter mentality. If we are going to rise to the urgency and challenge of our times, Klein urges, we need more skills and knowledge as well as vision – "about history, about how to change the political system, and even about how to change ourselves".

That word "even" doesn't really do justice to the importance of the change happening inside ourselves and I think Klein realises this when later in her book she emphasises the need to address her own "internal Trump", her own shadow. Analysing one's shadow may seem introspective but it complements political practice. The more you understand yourself, the more effective you can be in your activities. Political action and psychological health are complementary. Thoughtful activism and self-insight go together. Introspection is not just about developing individual psychological health but about tuning into something much larger, the evolving *zeitgeist* of this century.

"Yes" and lessons from Standing Rock

Klein writes admiringly about the active movements of the nineties such as the anti-globalisation protests at Seattle and Genoa and the Occupy initiatives, but what she has learned from them is that "NO is not enough". There has to be a YES – "yes to the 'yes'" – in the form of an alternative vision. Her book is an encouragement to begin thinking how this vision might take form.

She describes "the lessons from Standing Rock" in North Dakota when the "water protectors" gathered outside the Standing Rock Sioux Reservation to try to stop the Dakota Access pipeline. The company was determined to build the oil pipeline under Lake Oahe, the sole source of drinking water for the Standing Rock Sioux, as well as take it under the Missouri River, which provides drinking water for 17 million people. The tribal leaders argued, if the pipeline ruptured, their people would have no safe water and their sacred sites would be desecrated. The slogan went up: *Mni Wiconi* – "water is life".

In the end Trump reversed Obama's initial decision to deny the permit for the pipeline but this could not erase the original achievement and lessons learnt. December 5, 2016 was the

Sioux's "last stand" against the most violent state repression. Many arrived to stand with them, including a convoy of more than two thousand military veterans. When Klein joined them she found a network of camps comprising ten thousand people. It had developed into a community that was much more than just a resistance to the pipeline. In the words of Bull Allard, the official historian of the Standing Rock Sioux Tribe, it had become a school, not just here to protect the Earth and water but **"to help humanity answer its most pressing question: how to live with the Earth again, not against it"**.

For Klein and the many other non-indigenous supporters the Standing Rock community had shown them "A Path through Anger": "a way to deal with rage and grief that went beyond venting". Klein had thought the space for this lesson would come through universities or city halls but Standing Rock was where she discovered it, "in the camps' combination of reaction and contemplation, and in the constant learning-by-doing modelled by Brave Bull Allard and so many other leaders here".

The Leap

Klein's book is a clarion call to action. She is an engaging left of centre socialist but she is also aware of the need to go beyond the old Utopianism. From Rousseau through Marx to twentieth century socialism, utopian ideals have inspired revolution and reform but they are also flawed. A new Utopianism which "dares to dream" must learn from the old limitations. Her penultimate chapter is entitled "A Time to Leap. *Because small steps won't cut it*". On the one hand there is the single issue of life's very survival due to climate change and mass extinction, while on the other "a gang of scandal-plagued plutocrats" has seized control of the White House. In Canada the NDP party of the centre left has developed a "Leap Manifesto", which is printed at the end of Klein's book.

In the past progressive political movements have espoused unreal utopian dreams on the one hand and campaigned on a variety of valued but disconnected issues on the other, what Klein refers to as "siloed politics", whether it be climate change or particular environmental causes, jobs and employment, human or animal rights, welfare benefits and so on. In their general meetings in Canada, convened to discuss many of the different issues at the same time, "we emphasised the frame that showed how so many of our problems – and solutions – are interconnected, because the frame could be expanded in whatever place or community the vision was applied. What they needed were *integrated* solutions". The "leap", they also realised, would depend on people coming together round values, not policies.

The Left has always been in a double bind. It has progressive ideals but has historically defined itself in opposition to the right. Revolution has always needed an established order to rebel against. To that extent Left and Right are symbiotic, which is the dynamic that makes for history. Now we can visualise an actual end to history, evidenced by science, the urgent task is to find a way of understanding this symbiosis differently? Is there an "integrated solution" that understands Left and Right as some sort of unity, or at least frees the Left from its traditional co-dependency on the Right? What would it look like?

"Recovering environmentalism"

Paul Kingsnorth, who describes himself as "a recovering environmentalist" (see his book of essays by that title published this year) addressed the same problem in his own way in an extended essay in the *Guardian*, "The lie of the land: does environmentalism have a future in the age of Trump?" (18 March, 2017)

In the article Kingsnorth tells us he voted for Brexit. He didn't disclose this at the time, not because he didn't have good reasons for his voting decision but because of all the "mudslinging" going on and which he preferred to avoid. He is genuinely mystified why Greens and the left should have voted almost unanimously for "a multinational trading bloc backed by the world's banks, corporations and neoliberal politicians".

He writes, almost amusingly, about the surprise he experienced of waking up the morning after to discover unbelievably that the leave voters had won, an astonishment repeated at the election of Trump. Most interestingly he quotes Trump in his last TV spot before election victory: there is "a global power structure that is responsible for the economic decisions that have robbed our working class, stripped our country of its wealth and put that money into the pockets of a handful of large corporations and political entities". Whatever we make now of Trump saying this, it certainly weighed with the American electorate. As Kingsnorth comments: "they were words that could have been heard at any social forum, anti-globalisation gathering or left-green bean feast from the last 20 years, as could Trump's last rousing sentence: 'The only thing that can stop this corrupt machine is you'".

For Kingsnorth this was evidence that the anti-globalisation movement was not dead but moving in mysterious ways. In his *Guardian* essay he goes on to quote an article last year by Jonathan Haidt, "When and Why Nationalism Beats Globalism" in *The American Interest*, where Haidt suggests a new, or alternative, binary to the left/right political tradition of the last three hundred years. "Nationalism" Kingsnorth explains, "in the broadest sense of the term, was the default worldview of most people at most times, especially in most traditional places. It was a community-focussed attitude, in which a nation, tribe or ethnic group was seen as a thing to be loved and protected (the quality of life the Standing Rock Sioux community stood for). Globalism, the ideology of the rising urban bourgeoisie, was more individualistic. It valued diversity and change, prioritised rights over obligations and saw the world as a whole, rather than particular parts of it, as the moral community to which we all belong".

Belonging

Trump stoked the worst side of nationalism, the angry, prejudiced, intolerant form. But there is another way of looking at it. As Kingsnorth says: "What Haidt calls nationalism is really a new name for a much older impulse: the need to belong. Specifically, the need to belong to a place in which you feel at home". The anxiety about the increase in immigration may be more about this fear of losing a sense of secure identity than bigotry and prejudice towards foreigners. The globalists seem to have ignored this distinction.

The new populism, which the far right seem to have successfully harnessed for their own neoliberal interests, is evidence less of an economic than cultural wound at the heart of Western civilisation and which the globalists have not understood: "What is driving the modern turmoil are threats to identity, culture and meaning. Waves of migration, multicultural policies, eroding borders, shifting national and ethnic identities, global attacks on western culture: all that is solid melts into air". It is the Right who promise, however speciously, the return of that solidity, not the Left.

As Ken Wilber writes in his book on Trump, "worldcentric" globalism, as a cultural rather than economic phenomenon, demonstrates an advanced, more evolved form of cultural consciousness than modernity or traditional forms. But if it separates itself off from the main body of humanity and, worse, looks down contemptuously on them, then it leaves the way clear for the alternative Right to move in. Globalism is seen by many to be too elitist, too tied to narrow identity politics, and enthusiastic about breaking everything down, from gender identities to racial distinctions to national borders, while at the same time regarding any dissent as prejudice or hatred.

Global and local

Brexit and the defeat of Hilary Clinton provide important lessons for the globalists about how to remain true to a new global and ecological consciousness while staying empathetically in touch with the general electorate. The old maxim the Greens embraced from the 1970s on was to think globally while acting locally, but it seems to have been forgotten today. It is a timeless principle which comes out of the neo-platonic, mystical and ageless wisdom, as the One and the Many. Not everybody can see the big picture but the interconnectedness is everywhere if we look for it.

As Paul Kingsnorth suggests, the anti-globalist attack on the Greens is "a wake-up call. It points to the fact that green ideas have too often become a virtue signal for the carbon-heavy bourgeoisie, drinking their fair-trade coffee as they wait for their transatlantic flight. Green globalism has become part of the growth machine; a comfortable notion for those who don't really want much to change." We might do well to ask what a benevolent green nationalism would look like, the importance of the principle of acting locally in addition to thinking globally.

There is no one answer to this. Kingsnorth goes on to offer up one piece of advice from all his years of environmental campaigning: "any attempt to protect nature from the worst human depredation has to speak to people where they are". The natural world should not be "an obstacle in the way of our progress but a part of our community that we should nurture. That is part of our birthright." The challenge is how to be both global and local. That requires vision, a vision which Naomi Klein and the Left are beginning to think about.

Before that, perhaps we first have to address the issue of anger – not just at Trump, complacent globalist greens, or the fact of climate change denial, but our own, often objectless anger. Perhaps we need to understand where that comes from within ourselves. Naomi Klein's righteous anger shines through in all her writing. Anger is a natural emotion but doesn't have to be destructively acted out. Hence the importance of getting to know it and learn what it can tell us about ourselves.

PANKAJ MISHRA: Understanding anger

On the opening page of Pankaj Mishra's *Age of Anger,* by way of an epigraph, is a 1922 quote from the Hungarian sociologist, Karl Mannheim:

> Everywhere people are awaiting a messiah, and the air is laden with the promises of large and small prophets.... we all share the same fate: we carry within us more love, and above all more longing than today's society is able to satisfy. We have all ripened for something, and there is none to harvest the fruit.

Mishra's book is the story of the flawed attempts throughout European and world history to satisfy that longing and bring in the harvest. (See also an article, "Welcome to the age of anger", by Mishra, *Guardian* December 8 2016). The anger and *ressentiment* he writes about, as a result of that failure have reached incandescent levels today across the whole world. It is not clear that we have begun to recognise, let alone understand this. In his introductory chapter he quotes an anonymous contributor to the *New York Review of Books*, who is convinced that the West cannot, for instance, "ever develop sufficient knowledge, rigour, imagination, and humility to grasp the phenomenon of ISIS".

Although the bibliographic essay at the end of the book testifies to Mishra's intellectual credentials, it is primarily the texts and lives of poets, novelists and imaginative writers that he draws on to make his case. Shelley famously called poets "the unacknowledged legislators of mankind" but, of course, they also help us understand and interpret any age – Homer for Greece, Virgil for Rome, Dante for medieval Europe, Milton for reformation Europe, and so on. Mishra's book is "not offered as an intellectual history", nor a straightforward cultural narrative of the rise of *ressentiment* in the last two hundred years, rather "it explores a particular *climate* of ideas, a structure of feeling, and cognitive disposition, from the age of Rousseau to our own age of anger".

Our sense of bewilderment today was never greater. Mishra catches our perplexity, for instance, at the hands of terrorist movements such as Al Qaeda and ISIS:

> Attacks on Western cities since 9/11 have repeatedly provoked the questions: "Why do they hate us? " and "Who are *they*?" Before the advent of Donald Trump, the Islamic State of Iraq and Syria (ISIS) deepened a sense of extraordinary crisis in the West with

> its swift military victories, its exhibitionist
> brutality, and its brisk seduction of young
> people from the cities of Europe and America.

ISIS seems even more perplexing than Al Qaeda was. Why, for instance, has "Tunisia, the most Westernised among Muslim countries and where the 'Arab Spring' originated, sent such a large contingent of foreign jihadis to Iraq and Syria?" Why have dozens of British women, "including high achieving schoolgirls", joined up to marry men who have enslaved and raped girls as young as ten years old? The anonymous writer in *The New York Review of Books* declared "we should admit that we are not only horrified but baffled..... Nothing since the triumph of the Vandals in Roman North Africa has seemed so sudden, incomprehensible and difficult to reverse".

Ressentiment

Assaulted, as we are, by "grisly images and sounds" in this age of anger, "the threshold of atrocity has been steadily lowered since the first televised beheading in Iraq of a Western hostage dressed in Guantanamo's orange jumpsuit" while, at the same time, the racism and misogyny continuously displayed in social media and increasing demagoguery in politics serve to reveal what Nietzsche, speaking of the "men of *ressentiment*", called "a whole tremulous realm of subterranean revenge, inexhaustible and insatiable in outbursts". Hannah Arendt wrote of "negative solidarity", a "tremendous increase in mutual hatred and a somewhat universal irritability of everybody against everybody else". As Mishra observes, in a climate of "pervasive panic", generated and amplified by the news media, as well as by social media, anything seems to be able to happen anywhere to anybody at any time: "The sense of a world spinning out of control is aggravated by the reality of climate change, which makes the planet itself seem under siege from ourselves".

In writing of a universal crisis Mishra shifts the burden of responsibility of explanation from Islam and religious extremism and focuses on our own political, economic and social disorder accompanying the rise of the industrial capitalist economy in nineteenth century Europe, which led to totalitarian regimes and genocide in the first half of the twentieth century and is now "infecting much larger regions and bigger populations". These were first exposed to modernity through European imperialism but "larger parts of Asia and Africa are now plunging deeper into the West's own fateful experience of that modernity".

There has been increasing critical awareness of the limitations of what has come to be dubbed "the Enlightenment project", whether through the analyses of the Frankfurt (and neo-Frankfurt) School or the writings of political philosophers such as Isaiah Berlin or John Gray, who wrote the classic *Enlightenment's Wake: Politics and Culture at the Close of the Modern Age* (2007). In his book *Al Qaeda and What It Means to be Modern* (2003) Gray identified Al Qaeda as a product of modernity and of globalisation rather than an Islamic phenomenon. Mishra, with his Far-Eastern perspective, expressed in his recent *From the Ruins of Empire: the Revolt Against the West and the Remaking of Asia* (2013) sees it even more clearly: "the history of modernisation is largely one of carnage and bedlam rather than peaceful convergence, and the politics of violence, hysteria and despair was by no means unique to Nazi Germany, Fascist Italy or Communist Russia".

Moreover, the prosperity and sustained economic growth that made for peaceful social democracy in the West after the Second World War "helped obscure deeper disruptions and longer traumas". We ignored these, or were unaware of them: "The sanitised histories celebrating how the Enlightenment or Great Britain or the West made the modern world put the two world wars in a separate quarantine box, and isolated

Stalinism, Fascism and Nazism within the mainstream of European history as monstrous aberrations" rather than see them for what they were: a part of our own shadow.

"Totalitarianism", with all its horrors, was viewed as an evil reaction to a benevolent Enlightenment tradition of rationalism, humanism, universalism and liberal democracy:

> It was clearly too disconcerting to
> acknowledge that totalitarian politics
> crystallised the ideological currents (scientific
> racism, jingoistic nationalism, imperialism,
> technicism, aestheticized politics, utopianism,
> social engineering and the violent struggle for
> existence) that flowed through all of Europe
> in the late nineteenth century.

The promises of the Western world

There are two ways of viewing the Enlightenment which, for Mishra, were embodied by a decadent Voltaire on the one hand and "the prickly and awkward" outsider, Rousseau, on the other. Voltaire died before seeing what happened in the Revolution but championed the ideals of the French *philosophes*, particularly their rationalism, freedom from religious authoritarianism and belief in progress. Rousseau denounced modern commercial society for its moral corruption and inequality. He denied the enlightenment assumption of unending progress in human affairs, warning, in Mishra's words, "that a civilisation built upon endless competition, desire and vanity deforms something valuable in natural man: his simple contentment and unselfconscious self love".

Even Dostoevsky sensed the "unnerving appeal of the new materialist civilisation and its accompanying ideology of individualism" as it was expressed in Prince Albert's great project, the Crystal Palace. Dostoevsky wrote: "You become aware of a colossal idea; you sense that here something has been achieved, that here there is victory and triumph". But the great Russian novelist was not fooled, even as he watched millions of people coming from all over the world to worship, as it were, at this shrine of materialism:

> ... you feel that something final has taken place here, that something has come to an end. It is like a Biblical picture, something out of Babylon, a prophecy from the Apocalypse coming to pass before your eyes. You sense

> that it would require great and everlasting
> spiritual denial and fortitude in order not
> to submit, not to capitulate before the
> impression, not to bow to what is, and not to
> deify Baal, that is, not to accept the material
> world as your ideal.

The Enlightenment and the achievements of modernity have promised much by way of material progress but have failed to deliver to the majority of the population. Hence the rise of *ressentiment* in its wake. In the eighteenth century it was a progress only delivered to the ruling class and led to the French Revolution. In the nineteenth it was at the expense of an immiserated urban working class and led to nationalist uprising and a century of revolution. In the twentieth it led to Empires clashing in a century of world war and genocide, with the slaughter of over 100 million people. In the twenty-first it has resulted in a "global civil war" and put the earth and all its life at risk of mass extinction. It should come as no surprise that the world is ablaze with anger, envy, resentment, and hatred.

In short, the promises of Western capitalism have encouraged world populations in a mimetic desire of a material, consumer and unachievable way of life, while at the same time, through an increasingly heartless market ideology, depriving them of the natural cultural consolations they had cultivated in their societies over centuries, even thousands of years.

Mishra comes from a traditional way of life and witnessed the loss that his parents experienced through the adoption nationally of modern market mechanisms. He acknowledges that he is "a stepchild of the West" and has benefitted from the achievements of the Enlightenment and modernity but is also witness to what it has done to the developing world, particularly in the East. In shifting the focus of our attention from irrational and bigoted Islamophobia he asks us to look at the shadow in our own imperialist past, much, perhaps, the same way we might reconsider the reality of slavery in the history of the European Enlightenment and the modern world.

Slavery and slave labour

We are apt to forget that Ancient Greece and Rome, which are the foundations of European civilisation, were slave societies, whose culture of democracy, freedom and the rule of law were built on the work of an unfree and oppressed majority class. Mishra doesn't quote him but Ta-Nehisi Coates, whose National Book Award winner, *Between the*

World and Me (2015), Toni Morrison insisted was "required reading", has written with eloquent anger to remind us that European and American civilisation was built on slavery and slave labour and that Trump, as the "first White President", has shown us that race remains a strong force in 21st century North American society.

"White Supremacy" has now stepped out of the shadows and revealed itself for what it is. Trump represents those who could never accept a "n....." in the White House and hate Obama the more for showing us that an urbane, educated black man, married to an equally intelligent and educated black woman, can govern as well as any white man. We should remember that the election of Obama was a great American achievement and nothing Trump does can ever ultimately erase the reality of that achievement. Coates' latest book, *Eight Years in Power, An American Tragedy (2017)* documents Obama's achievement. Morrison has called him the new James Baldwin. Coates is a regular contributor to *The Atlantic* where he wrote his extended article on Trump as "The First White President". He also more recently wrote an article this year in the *Guardian*, "We should have seen Trump coming" (September 29).

WHERE HAS TRUTH GONE?

The truth about ourselves

If we really think about where the truth has gone, we will realise it hasn't gone anywhere. It's just that we don't see, or have lost sight of it. The main theme of truth is the truth about ourselves, who and what we are, as essentially a form of consciousness or awareness. Mishra seems unwilling, or unable, to draw on the wisdom of his ancient Indian culture. He knows about his Hindu and Buddhist wisdom traditions – he did write a personal account of Buddhism, *The End of Suffering: the Buddha in the World* (2004) – but it as if, like India itself, he is somehow blocked from drawing on them. It's as if his anger has to be dealt with first.

Anger is not a negative feeling. If we use our emotional intelligence to try to understand it, then we will find wisdom. Otherwise it turns into hatred and violence. At the end of his epilogue, *Finding Reality,* Mishra concludes that the appeal of radical Islamists, like other demagogues, comes from "a deeply felt incoherence of concepts", which leaves individuals isolated, confused and fearful and which our own ideological incoherence only exacerbates. Checking the expansion and appeal of a phenomenon like ISIS is not just a military task. It also requires the articulation of an alternative intellectual and moral case, argued with clarity and conviction.

The election of Donald Trump has highlighted the chasm, first explored, as Mishra points out, by Rousseau, between "an elite which seizes modernity's choicest fruits" and the mass of people who, denied of those fruits, "recoil into cultural supremacism, populism and rancorous brutality". The contradictions and costs of that elite's progress are now to be seen on a planetary scale. Mishra finally concludes:

> They (the contradictions and costs) encourage
> the suspicion – potentially lethal among the
> hundred of millions of people condemned
> to superfluousness – that the present
> order, democratic or authoritarian, is built
> upon force and fraud; they incite a broader
> and more apocalyptic mood than we have
> witnessed before. They also underscore the
> need for some truly transformative thinking
> about both the self and the world.

This is where Ken Wilber picks up. The ancient and perennial wisdom of the Far East has migrated to the West.

KEN WILBER'S BIG PICTURE

Ken Wilber has been described as a national treasure in the

States. Given that his uncommon books have been translated into twenty or more languages, he might equally be considered a global treasure. He is not so well known or recognised in the U.K. and it is difficult to find his work in our bookshops; nor is he cited by British writers, though I imagine he is read seriously by some, even if he is not officially acknowledged. This would be understandable since he writes from the perennial – formerly thought to be the "esoteric" – tradition, outside the regular context of conventional or academic thinking.

I remember, some fifteen or so years ago, while browsing through the philosophy shelves in what was then Dillon's in London, coming across a copy of his major 850 page work, *Sex, Ecology, Spirituality: the Spirit of Evolution*, first published in 1995. I initially thought it was a book of new age obscurantism, until I looked through its contents and index sections and saw his 250 pages of notes and the 30 pages of references, which read like a Who's Who of all the world's great thinkers – and included a survey of the major figures in our modern and postmodern traditions. He seemed, as I later realised, eminently qualified to write *A Brief History of Everything* (1996), the shorter follow-up to *SES*.

111

For Wilber to write a short topical book on Trump, which grew out of an online essay as an immediate response to the election result, is unusual but, like Klein and Mishra perhaps, he wanted to take the opportunity of this dramatic turn of events to comment urgently from the perspective of his own thinking. He does summarise that thinking in the second chapter of *Trump*, but his ideas have emerged over almost forty years since he published his first book, *The Spectrum of Consciousness*, (1977). Some knowledge of his writing might make it easier to appreciate his thought.

For instance he uses terms which may be unfamiliar to people, such as "AQAL" ("All Quadrants, All Levels") and "Integral Metatheory". AQAL refers to a mandala-like diagram to be found in *Sex, Ecology, Spirituality* and *Brief History* which ingeniously illustrates how evolution – both of "matter" and mind – correspondingly unfolds in terms of levels – greater complexification – and the four quadrants of individual and collective forms in both their interior (intentional and cultural) and exterior (behavioural and social) manifestations. Integral Metatheory refers to his thesis that we have reached a qualitative turning point in human affairs where we must, and can, begin to think and act integratively, rather than purely analytically. This is not just a theory but also a practice that can be used in any sphere of human activity. Wilber also relates different developmental stages of cultural consciousness to a colour-coded system, a creative use of the rainbow spectrum to illuminate the evolution of the collective human mind. To me Wilber's perennial view provides just "the vision" Klein says is needed and "the truly transformative thinking" about self and the world Mishra asks for in these very uncertain, apocalyptic times.

In his preliminary *Note to the Reader* Wilber suggests that much of the vocal response to the election of Trump has missed "what is perhaps the single most central issue and crucial item for truly understanding what happened, why it did, and what it means". We need this understanding before we think about our response, particularly in a country like the United States where 50% of the people vehemently hate and are opposed outright to the other half and where "no such one can move forward with any sort of grace, dignity, and integrity". Wilber's book is an exploration which involves looking at "a centrally core process of being human .... a political analysis that is also a process of self discovery".

For Wilber "there is a bigger picture operating here" and he outlines this in his first chapter entitled "Self Correction at the Leading Edge". The pain and suffering that both halves of American society are experiencing is, Wilber contends, the result of identifying with too narrow a view. A more expansive stance offers genuine release, whichever side a person wishes to work on.

Cultural evolution and the green wave

Drawing on the original thinking of a German poet and cultural philosopher, Jean Gebser (who, incidentally, was a colleague at one time of Jung and Erich Neumann) Wilber has written extensively about cultural evolution in terms of the development of structures of consciousness – from archaic, physiological ("infrared") to magical, egocentric ("red") to mythic, ethnocentric ("amber") forms in earlier structures, to the later forms of modern scientific, rational, "worldcentric", or global, ("orange") consciousness to current more creative and intuitive ("green") structures. These are not just historical but go beyond history and can be seen as complex overlapping structures of consciousness that are often in evidence in all of us at any time. Nor are they just to be conceived as linear or serial in their development but as nested. None of the structures are separate and distinct. The more evolved build on the earlier. They both "transcend and include" them. Regression to earlier structures can, and does, occur, but ideally, and from an evolutionary perspective, they can also be integrated – as we are becoming more aware.

Wilber also maps structures of consciousness beyond green in all his writings. These are analysed psychologically in his book, *Integral Psychology* (2000), where he provides some twenty charts of his own extended basic structures and correlates them to the thought and writing of other thinkers and psychological researchers. They are not colour-coded there but they are, extensively, in *The Religion of Tomorrow* (2017). For instance Integral consciousness – which is the genuine post-modern – is referred to as "turquoise", and he sketches other levels beyond turquoise.

But he suggests "the leading edge of cultural evolution is today – and has been for four or five decades – the green wave". The green wave is not just an ecological perspective, it refers to the basic stage of human growth and development characterised as "pluralistic", "postmodern", "individualistic" in the sense of "self-actualising", encouraging of diversity, inclusiveness and multiculturalism, and so on. Wilber refers to it as "postmodern" to differentiate it from "modern" or "traditional". These three – "traditional", "modern" and "postmodern" – are the most populous value systems in the

West's historical and cultural thinking, and the tensions between them account for what have become known as "the culture wars".

The primary purpose of the leading edge of cultural evolution – today the green, postmodern wave – is to be just that, a leading edge, or what the social and psychological thinker, Abraham Maslow, called "a growing tip", pointing to new, novel, creative and adaptive areas of human development. The green wave, as a major cultural force, began in the 1960s and soon bypassed modern (orange). The modern, previous leading edge can be characterised as rational, scientific, analytical thinking, with an emphasis on progress and individual self-esteem.

Green started with a series of healthy and evolutionary positive movements – civil rights, environmental sustainability, personal and professional feminism, anti-hate-crime legislation, heightened sensitivity to all forms of social oppression, particularly for minorities and, importantly, the understanding of the crucial role of context and the social construction of reality in all knowledge claims. As Wilber notes, 3 per cent of the population was "at green" in 1959 whereas twenty years later, by 1979, it was 20 per cent.

"There is no truth"

But towards the end of the twentieth century "green increasingly began veering into extreme, maladroit, dysfunctional, even clearly unhealthy forms". Broad-minded pluralism slipped into runaway relativism and nihilism. The notion that all truth is contextualised turned into a belief that there is no real universal truth at all, only shifting interpretations of it. This eventually led to widespread narcissism. Central notions, which began as important "true but partial" concepts, "collapsed into extreme and deeply self-contradictory views". All knowledge was thought to be socially constructed, context-bound and with no privileged perspectives. Wilber summed up this trend – and it is perhaps worth quoting him at length to convey his general exasperation:

> What passes for "truth" is a cultural
> fashion and is always advanced by one
> oppressive force or another (racism, sexism,
> Eurocentrism, patriarchy, capitalism,
> consumerism, greed, environmental
> exploitation): each and every human
> being, often including animals, is utterly,
> absolutely of equal value (egalitarianism).
> If there were one line that summarises the

message of virtually all of the truly prominent postmodern writers (Jacques Derrida, Michael Foucault, Jean-Francois Lyotard, Pierre Bourdieu, Jacques Lacan, Paul de Man, Stanley Fish, etc.) it is that "there is no truth". Truth rather was a social construction and what any body actually called "truth" was simply what some culture somewhere had managed to convince its members was truth; but there was no actually existing, given, real thing called "truth" that is simply sitting around awaiting discovery, any more than there is a single universally correct hem length that it is clothes designers' job to discover. Even science itself was held to be no more true than poetry. (Seriously) There was simply no difference between fact and fiction, news and novels, data and fantasies. In short there was "no truth" anywhere.

As he added:

there is no universal moral framework – what is true for you is true for you, and what's true

for me is true for me – and neither of these
claims can be challenged on any grounds that
do not amount to oppression; the same is
true for value...

Every single truth and value are simply deconstructed, an approach that leads to extreme nihilism and narcissism. This extreme perspective, however, led the postmodernists to commit what the philosophers call a "performative contradiction". Wilber sums it up: "Their entire theory itself is a very Big Picture about why all Big Pictures are wrong, a very extensive meta narrative about why all meta narratives are oppressive". He implies that you cannot not have a big picture. To think you can is delusional.

In his book *Sex, Ecology, Spirituality* Wilber referred to this flaw in postmodern thinking as "aperspectival madness" – the belief that there is no truth – and concluded that when "it infects the leading edge of evolution, evolution's capacity for self direction and self-organisation is bound to collapse". It strikes me this is perhaps why we are so incensed – and at something of a loss – when Trump refers to the "fake news" of our liberal media. He is, as it were, the little boy pointing out that the emperor has no clothes. As Wilber stresses, the notion that there is no truth is "the theoretical foundation on which all the other cherished green extremisms rely", whether these are extreme egalitarianism, political correctness, absolutist social equality, denial of free speech, and so on. To quote Wilber again in his chapter on the lessons green must learn:

> The fact is that it is definitely not true that
> there is no truth – astonishingly enough, that
> fact has become fairly obvious, especially
> when its blatantly immediate ridiculousness
> has been made apparent by almost every
> word out of Trump's mouth. What absolutely
> no philosopher, no matter how great, has
> been able to do over the past four decades
> – not Habermas, not Taylor, none of them –
> Donald Trump managed to do within a month.
> Lord, when evolution self corrects, it really
> self corrects.

The legitimation crisis and cultural regression

Unwittingly perhaps, Trump is bringing us to our senses. We might add that the paramount truth that our scientists are claiming and so many people deny, as does Trump, is climate change and mass extinction.

Again unwittingly, Trump is bringing more of us to the realisation of this truth.

When the leading edge, who are supposed to be in charge and know where we are going, lose their way, as Wilber argues the green wave has – what he terms a "legitimation crisis" – then society is likely to regress to earlier structures of consciousness. Hence we see the election of a president who acts and thinks egocentrically and ethnocentrically. As Wilber points out, all Trump's instincts and actions are fundamentally "anti-green" – in Wilber's larger sense of "green" – whether in his envious antipathy to Obama or his sense of white national tribalism.

This also partly accounts for the upsurge of fundamentalism in the world. In his recent book, *Culture and the Death of God* (2015) Terry Eagleton makes the point, in a section on fundamentalism and late modernity, that the attack on the twin towers on September 11th, 2001, was a major wake up call for the West. He argues that, despite the "faithlessness of modern capitalism.... God has by no means vanished". Belief in some form of moral order may still be felt; indeed, "just at the point when Western capitalism may have been edging in this direction, two aircraft slammed into the World Trade Center and metaphysical ardour broke out afresh".

Unfortunately this did not cause us to stop and think about the meaning of 9/11 or reflect on our own collective shadow. Instead the decision was made to act out of equal anger and launch an illegal and barbaric invasion of Iraq.

Wilber divides his book into three parts – *An Overview, The Territory* and *The Immediate Future.* His first chapter, "Self-Correction at the Leading Edge", which I have explored so far, introduces the main themes. His second, "That Ever Expanding Stairway", is a very brief outline of his thinking on human evolutionary development, individually and socially. He then focusses on "The Birth of a Post-Truth Culture". In Part Two he explores *ressentiment* under the title "No Truth and No Jobs", discusses "The Reverberating Anti-Green Field" and, in chapter six, addresses "The Primary Cause – and Cure – of Oppression". In Part Three he asks "Where Do We Go from Here?", before discussing "Dominator Hierarchies and Growth Hierarchies" and "The Lessons Green Must Learn", then finishing in his final chapter by suggesting "Another Way Forward", which he is convinced must be "Truly Integral".

The Leading Edge

Hilary Clinton lost the election for many reasons. Yes, there was the anger about "no jobs", when the rich were seen to be looking after themselves, and the contempt felt to be coming from the elite – Clinton's infamous "basket of deplorables" phrase. And the lack of understanding about racial identity. But, perhaps also, in addition, there was the sense of a governing class which had lost its way and its legitimacy. Trump's time in office, whether four or eight years – assuming he's not impeached – may give the "leading edge" the chance to rethink and re-form. After all Bernie Sanders, the candidate with no corporate backing, offered a near "revolution" and "a Future to Believe In" while here in the UK Jeremy Corbyn proved in the recent UK election that social justice issues still count. Politics is important, as is the need to reach out somehow to the voters who put Trump in office and not condescend and demean them. But politicians are – or should be – only the executive arm of the Leading Edge. They are guided by all those of us who form our values, whether we are philosophers, religious and spiritual leaders, economists, scientists, musicians, poets, teachers, therapists and so on.

The noble prize-winning Belgian scientist, Ilya Prigogine and philosopher, Isabelle Stengers, published a landmark book, entitled *Order Out of Chaos,* in 1986 in which they argued that, according to chaos theory, even insentient material systems have an inherent drive to self-organisation. When physical systems find themselves pushed "far from equilibrium" they escape this chaos by leaping into a higher-level state of organised order. Since we – homo sapiens – are an integral part of nature and subject to cultural evolution, we should be asking why our leaders are not making that leap to avoid the disaster our climate scientists say awaits us.

If we are looking for the truth of the 21st century, we need the political analysis of Naomi Klein and Pankaj Mishra's understanding of the seeds of our own anger, but we also need the systemic and integral thinking, the bigger picture as outlined by Ken Wilber.

November 2017

Who Are We?
Identity in the Anthropocene

The human form is a microcosm of the
universe. All that supposedly exists outside us
in reality exists in us. The world is in you and
can become known in you, as you. What then
is this 'you'?

Jean Klein,
Who Am I? The Sacred Quest

I first came into contact with the Climate Psychology Alliance
(CPA) in 2011 at a Psychotherapy and Counselling for Social
Responsibility (PCSR) meeting in London addressed by
Clive Hamilton not long after he published *Requiem for a*

Species (2010), subtitled *Why We Resist the Truth about Climate Change*. Hamilton is Professor of Public Ethics at Canberra University. He gave a powerful presentation, reiterating the theme of *Requiem*: not just about the urgent need to raise the alarm and take radical action to head off climate chaos but asking why, at this late stage, we continue to ignore the warnings; why we remain in denial about global warming and the mass extinction going on all around us; why, in short, we appear so indifferent to our dying planet. The requiem note of sorrow and grief seemed to capture feelings more likely to get behind the defences of denial and avoidance we are trapped in. Clive Hamilton was inviting us to think about the unthinkable – the demise, if not of all life on the planet, of human civilisation as we know it – and what we feel about it.

His *Defiant Earth: the Fate of Humans in the Anthropocene* (2017), thoughtfully reviewed recently on the CPA website by Chris (Robertson), strikes an even more apocalyptic note, in addition to a sorrowful one. 'The Anthropocene Rupture' describes how modern man has interrupted the geological time scale, succinctly but also clearly described and analysed by the eco-socialist writer, Ian Angus in *Facing the Anthropocene: Fossil Capitalism and the Crisis of the Earth System* (2016). The Anthropocene apart, the next Ice Age was due in 50,000 years, potentially extending our stable and temperate Holocene epoch fourfold and, hopefully, giving us the time to evolve as responsible and enlightened stewards of the Planet. Instead we may be living in our final century since we emerged on Earth 200,000 years ago, condemning at the same time many fellow life forms that have evolved over millions. It would seem with our modern science we have become, in Hamilton's phrase, "hubris on steroids" and now are subject to the nemesis of a *Defiant Earth.*

Some are still hubristic enough to believe modern science can solve all our problems, can still master the planet. Others denounce the anthropocentrism leading us to this potential disaster, preferring to ignore both the impressive power we now have to destroy all life, but equally to protect and nurture it. Clive Hamilton asks in his book how "a new ethics" might lead us to act responsibly rather than destructively. In his last chapter, "The Rise and Fall of the Super-agent" he wonders, speculatively, "whether, in allowing humans free will, 'nature' made a colossal mistake". But earlier he had quoted the idealist German philosopher, Friedrich Schelling, that *freedom is woven into the fabric of nature,* suggesting that ethical freedom lies not outside and independent of nature, as modern scientific man believes, but within it. In his earlier books, *Growth Fetishism, Affluenza* and *The Freedom Paradox,* Hamilton has written extensively and critically about our compulsive consumerism and its failure to bring us happiness or freedom. In *The Freedom Paradox* he identifies our inner freedom as necessarily based in an ethical practice and he covers an impressive range of world thought to illustrate this. In *Defiant Earth* he now suggests that a new ethics "awaits the realisation that this being called human has become something strange and unfamiliar" and he wonders whether human beings will emerge who embody another future than the one we all most fear. He does not pretend to know exactly what this new "being" – "the new anthropocentrism" – would be like, though he is wary of any forms simply of the old transcendentalisms. *Defiant Earth* challenges us to think about this.

A new awareness

I would like to suggest that the contemplation of climate change – and the fact of our own collective transience – can bring a new knowledge about ourselves, what the ancient Greeks called *gnosis,* a knowledge which identifies the vital – or divine – spark in all of us. This may not save human civilisation but it could today breathe new life into psychology and transform our modern natural and human sciences. Future generations may be inheriting a very damaged world but is it not crucial we also bequeath them a new self-knowledge – a modern, or post-modern, *gnosis* – so as to strengthen their ability to face whatever the future brings? We surely owe them this.

Perhaps this is already happening. Despite the crude instincts of neoliberalism, there is a growing awareness of the value of a systemic and integral perspective in all our thinking, and a greater understanding of the principle that the whole is always more than the sum of the parts. This perspective promises to integrate many of our disciplines and activities. It could even at last begin to bring together the divided minds of science and the humanities – "The Two Cultures" – and might also lead to a renewal in this 21st century of existential and metaphysical realities we have long come to ignore, amounting, in short, to a neo-perennial philosophy.

What is missed in our linear way of thinking is that, from a systemic perspective, a small, apparently insignificant change can lead to major transformations. Chaos theory bears this out. It is the thermostat principle. The slightest adjustment of the thermostat affects the whole heating system. We know this from our new climate knowledge. Change the ratio of the greenhouse gases in the atmosphere, which control our global temperature, and you move from the Holocene into the Anthropocene. This leads to all the dangers of our age but, if we are wise, it can also work in our favour. If we readjust the thermostat, who knows what changes this may in turn bring about? Are we, ourselves, the new thermostat for our warming globe? There may be no going back to the Holocene, but perhaps we can make more of the Anthropocene than the current despair or pessimism allow. Rather than any technological project of geo-engineering, perhaps a new understanding and awareness of ourselves is the thermostat that most needs adjusting.

Two of the illusions we cling to that are being seriously challenged, in both the modern natural and human sciences, are the notions of an absolute objective, common sense world "out there" on the one hand and the separate, autonomous individual self "in here" on the other. One might be thought to be an ontological or philosophical problem, the other an epistemological or psychological one. But they are very much related. Some of us may understand this cognitively but, more crucially, do we have an affective appreciation of it? Do we feel it? If the neoliberal assumption of the possessive individual person derives from the feeling, belief and experience of the world as fixed and solid, to break the spell of solidity must lead to a changed experience of ourselves.

"Objective" science.

In the introduction to *The Nature of the Physical World*, published in 1928, the physicist, Arthur Eddington, described the "two tables" in his study – one, a practical table that appears made of hard and long-lasting wood on which his books and his tea pot can reliably rest. This is the "empirical table". The other is the "scientific table", composed of trillions of atoms and molecules which are mostly space – emptiness – and lack the apparent and substantial boundaries the empirical table has. As Eddington and his colleagues were well aware, the quantum revolution questioned whether things are really what they appear to be. Science and common sense seemed to have diverged alarmingly. What we take to be substantial is only apparently so.

The revolution in physics at the beginning of the last century is well known, though as Richard Feynman has famously quipped, anyone who thinks he understands quantum mechanics clearly hasn't. As Ken Wilber notes in the introduction to his anthology, *Quantum Questions: Mystical Writings of the World's Great Physicists* (2001), what is less well-known is that Eddington and many of his more famous colleagues were, if not religious in the sense of conventional believers in God, mystically-minded men who accepted that the universe was essentially mysterious and not accessible to empirical or human rational thinking. In their view any relative hypotheses and theories they might make about the nature of the universe could never give them absolute knowledge of it. Physics is physics, not metaphysics. As Eddington reminded us physics may use the symbolic and beautiful language of mathematics to describe the world but it does not go beyond symbols:

> We should suspect an intention to reduce
> God to a system of differential equations...
> We have learnt that the exploration of the
> external world by the methods of physical
> science leads not to a concrete reality but to
> a shadow world of symbols, beneath which
> those methods are unadapted for penetrating.

It's almost as if, in declaring this, Eddington was suggesting that science was, in an important way, growing up. He was aware of the revolutionary breakthroughs his colleagues were making in their understanding of 'matter' but also aware that this was an understanding of the world as we represented it. These were only shadow symbols. Scientists were still all-too-human after all.

Two significant implications might be drawn from these breakthroughs. Firstly that any knowledge we have about the nature of the world depends on our human perspective, as well as the means by which we observe that world – whether we rely on our physical senses mainly, or our minds in addition to our senses. What is often missed, when we think about the wonders of science, is also the wonder of the human animal making those discoveries. Science may be one of our most impressive arts.

Practical mysticism

Secondly the human mind may have other ways, or paths, of gaining access to knowledge than purely rational, or even intuitional, thinking, something which our social and psychological sciences have forgotten, particularly when it comes to ultimate or absolute knowledge. The physicists of that revolutionary period in the first decades of the twentieth century were open-minded about the importance and value of metaphysics, and respectful of the sense of wonder the mystical traditions cultivated.

Contemporaneous with the revolution in physics came the publication of a comprehensive book narrating and illuminating the history of the mystical tradition in our European culture. Writing in the Preface to the twelfth edition of *Mysticism: A Study in the Nature and Development of Mankind's Spiritual Consciousness* (1911) in 1930, Evelyn Underhill, its author, wrote:

> Since this book first appeared
> nineteen years ago, the study of
> mysticism – not only in England but
> also in France, Germany and Italy –
> has been almost completely transformed.
> From being regarded, whether critically
> or favourably, as a by-way of religion,
> it is now more generally accepted by
> theologians, philosophers and psychologists,
> as representing in its intensive form the
> essential religious experience of man.

This statement of hers, coupled with the beliefs of the physicists, suggests that, in the twentieth century mysticism was beginning to be accepted as a true metaphysical science and no longer the persecuted heresy of the Church or simply the vague and misty fantasy modern natural science assumed it to be.

Mystics are traditionally conceived as set apart from the world, seeking knowledge of a transcendent power experienced in themselves as an immanent reality. But Underhill also emphasised both the practical side of mysticism and its usefulness for everyone. "Mysticism is the art of union with reality" she explained in a short, very readable book, *Practical Mysticism,* published in the first weeks of The Great War (1914, recently republished 2011), and "the mystic is the person who has attained that union in greater or less degree". "Union" can mean many things to many people – union with God, nature, or one's fellow human beings – or all these together. Underhill's "unitive life" is open to us all.

The First World War may have been an unprecedented occasion of mass carnage and slaughter but it was also a time of great social, cultural and spiritual ferment. In her preface to *Practical Mysticism* Evelyn Underhill writes that the mystical connection with reality is often intensified in times of distress and suffering:

> the stronger the forces of destruction
> appeared the more intense grew the spiritual
> vision which opposed them...the mystical
> consciousness has the power of lifting those
> who possess it to a plane of reality which no
> struggle, no cruelty can disturb: of conferring
> a certitude which no catastrophe can wreck.

Many people felt more vitally alive during the Wars, whether because of the proximity of death or the greater social connection they felt with each other.

Could it be that when we come to accept the peril that our scientists say awaits us, we will find solace and strength in the contemplative and mystical traditions?

Modernity has rightly turned its critical and analytic gaze on the more sentimental and naive aspects of Christian and Romantic mysticism. But to reject the notion of a mythic Heavenly Father who created the universe out of nothing is not to deny a God who is the ground of all being. Nor should we turn our backs on the Romantic revolution's feeling for transcendent and universal values.

The notion of the human soul has also fallen into disuse in our human sciences. Psychology, after all, was originally an enquiry into the nature of the soul. Perhaps it's time we brought the soul back.

Perhaps it needs redefining. Perhaps in the modern world it has been too identified with the notion of the individual mind rather than a quality of awareness we enjoy and share with everything. In his famous essay, "The Over-Soul", the great American transcendentalist, Ralph Waldo Emerson, described it as "a deep power in which we live":

> Within man is the soul of the whole; the wise
> silence; the universal beauty, to which every
> part and particle is equally related; the eternal
> ONE... We see the world piece by piece, as
> the sun, the moon, the animal, the tree; but
> the whole, of which these are the shining
> parts, is the soul.

Emerson echoes the perennial wisdom of ancient India.

Gnosis from the East

In the cultures of the Asian east mystics have been revered

and followed, albeit often uncritically. But this is not to discount the real wisdom their traditions offer. In the Indian *Vedas*, the sacred Hindu scriptures which are six times more extensive than the Bible, are to be found a kernel of profound philosophical and psychological teachings, consisting of some two hundred *Upanishads*. These were recognised as part of a world-wide intellectual and spiritual illumination in the middle of the first millennium BCE – the *Upanishads* and teachings of Gautama Buddha in India, the Taoism of Lao Tzu and, later, Chang Tzu in China, the Old Testament prophets in the Middle East and the Pre-Socratics in Ancient Greece – which Karl Jaspers in *The Origin and Goal of History* called "The Axial Age". People wonder whether we are now, in the 21st century – unbelievably, given the shadow side of the Anthropocene – entering a new axial age.

"Upanishad" means "sitting at the feet of" a guru, or "rishi", a contemplative teacher who is said to reveal the profound secrets of the universe. The *Upanishads* form the final portion of the revealed part of the *Vedas* and are the principal basis of Vedanta – the "conclusion" of the *Vedas* – and the most profound teachings of the Hindu tradition. They are said to be valued by wisdom seekers for their transcendent breadth and powerful freedom of thought.

Central to the Vedanta tradition are two related principles. The Sanskrit word a*tman* refers to the belief in the real immortal self of human beings, similar to our belief in the soul, while *brahman*, with which *atman* is identified, is a concept for which we in the modern West, with our dualistic thinking and belief either in a personal God or no God at all, have no equivalent. It refers to an Absolute which, in the *Upanishads,* is known as "eternal and imperishable". This is an abstract concept, and, being nameless and formless, beyond the experience of the knowing mind. Another way of putting it is that it is not an object of knowledge but what we essentially are, our very being.

This may be difficult for us to follow. Nor is it easy to read the *Upanishads.* W. B. Yeats, who, with Shree Purohit Swami, gave us a poetic rendering into english in 1937, was incredulous at how unreadable the original translations were: "Could latinised words, hyphenated words; could polyglot phrases, sedentary distortions of unnatural English: – 'However many Gods in Thee, All-Knower, adversely slay desires of a person' – could muddles, muddied by 'Lo! Verily' and 'Forsooth' represent what grass farmers sang thousands of years ago, what their descendants sing today?" Perhaps these unreadable translations reflect our original difficulties in understanding ancient texts we were encountering for the first time. Despite our difficulties, Yeats in his introduction was clear about the poetic and philosophic importance of the *Upanishads* for our time:

> Whatever the date, those forest Sages
> began everything; no fundamental problem
> of philosophy, nothing that has disturbed
> the schools to controversy, escaped their
> notice... It pleases me to fancy that a system
> of thought like that of these books...once
> overspread the world, as ours today; that our
> genuflections discover in the East something
> ancestral in ourselves, something we must
> bring into the light before we can appease a
> religious instinct that for the first time in our
> civilisation demands the satisfaction of the
> whole man.

Modern psychology

The practice, if not the theory, of modern psychology – whether cognitive, psychoanalytic, or humanist – is premised on the fundamental sense of the distinct, separate, finitely defined individual person and, in that, it lacks a systemic perspective. A non-systemic approach also emphasises the notion of separate subjects and professions. In the early nineties I did a training in family group and systemic psychotherapy at the Cardiff Family Institute in the UK, where they taught a forward-looking and liberating form of interpersonal therapy. It was an integrative practice, based in what Gregory Bateson called "the ecology of mind" and in the fundamental principle of the unity underlying everything. Individuality, they impressed on us at Cardiff, emerged in relationship – "I" and "we" only make sense together. In other words, who a person is is initially conjoined with the family as the original and primary group. Subjectivity is intersubjectivity.

The family cannot be conceived separate from society – it is essentially social and political. Nor can it either be separated from wider and more universal contexts. As Ken Wilber might say, a person may be egocentric, but his egocentricity leads to ethnocentric, "worldcentric", even "Kosmocentric" realities, all nested in each other. And the practice in Cardiff of working with family networks – as well as individuals – and analysing related social and political perspectives, mirrored their eco-systemic premises.

Perhaps surprisingly, Freud also theoretically recognised this truth. In her introduction to *Mass Psychology and Other Writings* (2004) (*Group Psychology* in Strachey's Standard Edition*)* in the new Penguin Modern Classics translations of Freud, edited by Adam Phillips, Jacqueline Rose questions 'the commonplace assumption that psychoanalysis only deals with individuals'.

Freud himself pointed out, in the first paragraph of *Mass Psychology*, that without the presence of the other there can be no mental life:

> The antithesis between the individual and
> social or mass psychology which at first
> glance may seem to us very important,
> loses a great deal of its sharpness on close
> examination.

And, interestingly, Rose comments: "We only exist through the others who make up the storehouse of the mind....The mind is a palimpsest in which the traces of these figures will jostle and arrange themselves for evermore. From the earliest moments of our lives.....we are 'peopled' by others. Our psyche is a social space."

It's helpful to remember that Freud was always developing his ideas, consciously or unconsciously, and that psychoanalysis itself was evolving, alongside other psychologies and cultural formations. The difference between the first and second halves of the twentieth century can be gauged, for instance, in the development of thinking between Freud and Jacques Lacan.

Unlike Freud, Lacan was notoriously obscure. but his notion of the three orders of the "Imaginary", "Symbolic" and "Real" turned psychoanalysis inside out, as it were. By defining the individual person as imaginary or "fictive", and language, like the unconscious, as something that lives us rather than something we have complete control over, Lacan offered a more developed interpretation of Freud's central concept – "the unconscious".

Interestingly, Lacan's concept of the three orders was known to the Tibetans a thousand years ago, for whom the Real was the essential and ultimate meta-physical reality. And Buddhism has always taught that a person is not a separate, autonomous individual. Hence its notion of *anatman,* or no-self. *Anatman* doesn't deny a self, only that we shouldn't limit it to the personal self.

The Self of the *Upanishads*

The *Upanishads* conceived a greater sense of self than the individual self, which can be described in an infinite number of ways. In Vedanta it is known as *atman-brahman*, while buddhists call it "buddha (or awakened) nature". Realising – making real – "Self", in addition to the personal self, may be as important in these apocalyptic times as our activism to reduce carbon emissions. Perhaps climate psychology is as much about redefining the self as the importance of de-carbonising society.

All the *Upanishads* return again and again to this theme of realising the true – or unconscious – self. In Eknath Easwaran's more accessible Arkana translation (1988), for instance, he gives the *Kena Upanishad* the title "Who Moves the World?" The *Kena* looks beyond the mind:

> *The student inquires:*
> "Who makes my mind think?
> Who fills my body with vitality?
> Who causes my tongue to speak? Who is that
> Invisible one who sees through my eyes
> And hears through my ears?"

The teacher replies:
"The Self is the ear of the ear,
  the eye of the eye, the mind of the mind,
  the word of words, and the life of life.
  Rising above the senses and the mind
  And renouncing separate existence,
  The wise realise the deathless Self."

In the resonant refrain of the *Chandogya Upanishad*, *You Are That*, "That" is the Self. The Self is "you". The "Self" is also viewed as the whole universe, the Life and Spirit within all things – *brahman*. Therefore, in this sense, "you" <u>are</u> the universe. Wordsworth had a feeling for this in nature when he wrote his *Lines Composed a Few Miles Above Tintern Abbey* (1798):

... For I have learned
  To look on nature, not as in the hour
  Of thoughtless youth, but hearing often
  The still sad music of humanity...
  ... And I have felt
  A presence that disturbs me with the joy
  Of elevated thoughts; a sense sublime
  Of something far more deeply interfused,

Whose dwelling is the light of setting suns,
And the round ocean and the living air
And in the blue sky, and in the mind of man:
A motion and a spirit, that impels,
All thinking things, all objects of all thought,
And rolls through all things...

The *Upanishads* and Buddhist texts were only just available in Latin translation in Wordsworth's time, unlike today when there are many english translations available. *The Isha Upanishad* – "The Inner Ruler" (Easwaran) – describes the Self in only eighteen verses but it catches the mystery with poetry that speaks across the millennia. In Yeat's words:

The Self is one. Unmoving, it moves faster than the mind. The senses lag, but Self runs ahead.
Unmoving, it outruns pursuit.
Out of Self comes the breath that is the life of all things.
Unmoving, it moves; is far away, yet near; within all, outside all.
Of a certainty the man who can see all creatures in himself, himself in all creatures, knows no sorrow.
How can a wise man, knowing the unity of life,

> seeing all creatures in himself, be deluded or
> sorrowful?
> The Self is everywhere, without a body, without a
> shape whole, pure, wise, all knowing, far shining,
> self-depending, all transcending; in the eternal
> procession assigning every period its proper duty.

Easwaran translates that last line: "He (Self) it is Who holds the cosmos together."

A twentieth century sage

The spirit of the *Upanishads* has found expression throughout the centuries. In the East Asian traditions there have been many understandings of the immaterial self, while in the West we have focused on the material self. In the nondual, *advaita* – "not-two" – tradition material and immaterial are a continuum, linked by the thread of consciousness that runs through both.

It is thought that the revival in the West in the last century of the nondual teachings of the East promise to unite the material and mind sciences of the West with the metaphysical idealism of the East. In 1896 a sixteen year-old schoolboy, named Venketerama, living at the tip of southern India, walked out on

his family and made his way to Arunachala, a holy mountain
and pilgrimage centre that he had always felt drawn to. On his
arrival he gave away all his money and possessions and, in the
words of David Godman, a later student of his, "abandoned
himself to a newly discovered awareness that his real nature
was formless, immanent consciousness". (Godman, *Be Who
You Are: The Teachings of Sri Ramana Maharshi.* (1983))

So intense was this awareness he just sat in silence for a number
of years in various caves on the mountainside, oblivious of his
body and the world. He neglected to eat and his hair and
fingernails grew to unmanageable proportions. Eventually
he began to look after his physical state but his awareness
of himself as consciousness remained undimmed for the rest
of his life. Godman explains: "In Hindu parlance he had
'**realised the Self**': that is to say, he had realised by direct
experience that nothing existed apart from an indivisible
and universal consciousness which was experienced in its
unmanifest form as beingness or awareness and in its manifest
form as the appearance of the universe."

After some years his inner awareness became an outer spiritual
radiance and attracted a small circle of followers, which grew
as the years passed until he eventually became quite famous,

not only in India but around the world. So impressed were other spiritual figures with the maturity of his wisdom that he was given the title Bhagawan Sri Ramana Maharshi. What attracted people to Ramana was not only his way of sharing his unassuming life and spiritual vitality with whoever came to see him but the simple and practical profundity of his teaching, which took the form of self-analysis, or personal inquiry, a contemplative practice which is potentially very effective in modern Western culture.

Hence the fundamental question, "Who Am I?", which forms the basis of his teaching to anyone who came to see him. It is the title of the opening chapter of *The Spiritual Teachings of Ramana Maharshi* (1988) – which has a foreword about Ramana by Jung, initially published as a foreword to Heinrich Zimmer's book, *Der Weg zum Selbst* (1913) – "The Path to the Self".

To inquire of oneself "Who Am I?" is based on the perennial Upanishadic principle of *neti, neti* – "not this, not this". It is the principle of negative discrimination or detachment, by which you distinguish the infinite number of "me"s from the one "I" which is asking the question – am I the named person, born in a certain time, in a particular place; someone with a national, racial and gender identity; a married, a professional person; someone of a certain age, ability, or inclination, etc? The answers to these questions provide a lot of information about oneself as "me", but do they amount to the "I" a person essentially is? Does this collection of "me"s add up to what "I" am? In the East what "I am" – the one essential assertion we can make about ourselves – is a changeless, timeless being and awareness, beyond any conditioning and objectification. In a Western culture the conditioned, contingent self is the one we mostly objectify and analyse.

Ramana asked people simply to continue asking this question, wherever they were or whatever they were doing. The more, it would seem, you understand who you are not, the nearer you come to the realisation of Self. From this perspective our psychologies, for instance, would seem to analyse and focus on who we are not. But, paradoxically, before you can be who you are, you need to know who you are not. And, then, who you are not – your contingent self – can be recognised also as an integral part of who you are. This is the paradoxical nondual way.

Ramana never wrote anything down but his many students made notes of his talks and their discussions with him. One student who wrote about him was the Englishman Arthur Osborn, and David Goldman was the later librarian of his ashram. The Frenchman, Jean Klein, taught in the tradition of *advaita* – nondual. The other famous 20th century Indian mystic, along with Ramana, was Sri Nisargadatta Maharaj, who was visited in his modest Bombay home by people from all over the world. In all his life Ramana never went further than two miles from his beloved mountain at Arunachala ever since he had arrived there as a teenager but, in his Foreword to the Inner Directions 2000 edition of his *Talks*, Wilber titles him as "the Sage of the Century".

In their preface to the 1988 edition of *The Spiritual Teaching* Joe and Guinevere Miller describe how free of doctrine or traditional meditation observances Ramana's teaching is and therefore how suited to our busy times:

> Beyond that which you think is that which you are. Realising this does not involve specific practices or attitudes other than Understanding. No withdrawal is necessary – no change of present time, place or condition – only a change of viewpoint, which you bring about yourself for your Self.

It is not possible to describe adequately what is beyond description. By simply acknowledging what you are not, the beauty of the nondual approach is that you are not losing yourself but gaining a freedom which leads you to be who you really are. The trick is simply to be aware of this and at the same time recognise that you are an integral part of everything and everyone else. This is the way of Evelyn Underhill's Union, the unitive path of all mystics, and the realisation of Self the Upanishads celebrated.

In conclusion: contemplating the abyss

In the age of the Anthropocene the problem, and the solution, as Clive Hamilton argues, surely lies with us, humanity. Naomi Klein, in the introduction to her book *This Changes Everything,* asks what is wrong with us that we seem to be doing nothing to help ourselves. One answer may be that we do not know who we are.

Or, as the mystics would say, we are not aware of who we are. The truth is we do not even know that we don't know who we are. This must be a central challenge for any social and psychological climate initiative. We dare not imagine what the world – this planet – will look like in 2100. Hence the resistance to thinking about climate change. We prefer to ignore or deny it. But as more people fear, we are looking into an abyss – a void – and for most of us that is a terrifying prospect. But the "abyss" – the "emptiness" – may hold the truth about ourselves. *Homo sapiens* – ourselves – is a mere 200,000 years old on a planet that goes back some 4.5 billion years. We are very transient. We are reluctant to think about this, but at the same time we have lost sight of what is timeless in us.

In the buddhist view "emptiness" – *shunyata* – is not empty in our sense of the word. It is a fullness. Another way of thinking about it is as the absolute interdependence of everything, and of ourselves as an interdependency rather than a finite, fixed species. Is it so difficult to contemplate that, as the product of the Earth, we may be said, in some way, to be as "old" as it, or even as the universe? That we have all of nature in our bodies and our minds, and all its history, even its future, written in us? Cosmologists say many of the elements in our bodies were forged in the stars. Is it too fanciful to imagine we even contain an image in our minds of the origin, mystery and future of the universe itself?

The great philosopher, Baruch Spinoza, advised we consider everything *sub specie aeternitatis* – in the light of eternity. He wasn't just pointing to an eternal universe out there, but to something timeless in us all. It falls to us in this Anthropocene Age to rediscover this. Whatever the turbulence and suffering to come, is it not an awareness we should bequeath to future generations?

May 2018

The New Axial Age: climate change and cultural evolution

I have been re-reading Bill McKibben's 1990 climate classic *The End of Nature,* along with *Eaarth: Making a Life on a Tough New Planet* (2010). Reading through the sobering message of *Eaarth* takes some recovering from – even more so five years after its publication! Matthew Nisbet hailed him as "Nature's Prophet" in a Shorenstein discussion paper, subtitled "Bill McKibben as Journalist, Public Intellectual and Activist" (March 2013). With his books, articles, campaigns and movements, such as 350.org and the fight against the Keystone XL oil pipeline, McKibben has arguably done more than anyone to wake us all up to the climate and ecological crisis we are facing and which we are responsible for. Also, being the most well known environmentalist on the planet, he gets a rockstar reception on intelligent chat shows, such as Bill Maher's *Real Time*. As he pointed out to his host on one occasion, in the face of devastating facts about what we are doing to the planet, the "silver lining" is that people are fighting back – in larger and larger numbers.

The End of Nature was as much religious and philosophical as ecological, and drew inspiration from the American transcendentalists and mystics such as Thoreau, Emerson and John Muir. As a practising Methodist, McKibben took a Romantic Christian view of nature, valuing wilderness and the sense in which God created a nature larger than man and where we could always retreat for solitude and consolation, a sense we have now lost since, with our science and technology, we have made it into a human rather than divine planet. We have desecrated the Earth, or as he wrote: *we have ended the thing that, at least in modern times, defined nature for us – its separation from human society* (his italics).

McKibben, prompted by his wife, Sue Halpern, also took an interest in the biblical story of Job, enough to write a book about him, The *Comforting Whirlwind: God, Job and the Scale of Creation* (2005). Job was a just and prosperous man, brought down by the devil who made a wager with God that, if Job lost his prosperity and happiness, he would curse God. The devil lost his wager. Job did not curse God but he did demand a meeting with Him and, in the famous passage of the book, God asks him with some pride: "Where were you when I laid the foundations of the Earth?" Job has no answer and accepts that in all innocence there is a limit to his knowledge and understanding. In McKibben's mind, today, with our over-weening pride, arrogance and blindness to our ignorance, we have lost touch with Job's suffering and humility. In our hubris, we have changed the face of the Earth and hence have moved from the stable and clement Holocene into the very uncertain Anthropocene.

It is possible to speculate that, had Job had the benefit of today's global scientific and cultural perspective, he might have been able to give an answer to God's presumptive question. Science, for instance, has shown that we carry around inside ourselves evidence of the whole of Earth's 4.5 billion years of history. Job might have answered, in that sense, he <u>was</u> there at "the foundations of the Earth" and would also have been entitled to inquire of God why He did not then see him. Which is not to say a twenty-first century Job would not also have retained his humility. He may have had a better grasp of the past than God but at the same time he would have conceded the future remained uncertain and unknown.

I agree that the issues about climate change are as much, if not more, about religion, philosophy and ethics as they are about economics and environmental ecology but I want to suggest that they are also about the most significant concept and truth of modern science – the fact and truth of evolution, not just biological but also religious and cultural evolution. The orthodoxy of the monotheistic religions no longer satisfies the leading edge of Western society today. But nor, if we are honest, do the cultural tenets of modernity. Neither a purely transcendent God nor an immanence based solely on self-centred human beings is sufficient. Could it be we are working towards a new spirit of integration? That the relationship between transcendence and immanence leads towards a new relationship between humanity and nature, or even between "heaven and earth"?

Science writing today

There is a new generation of science journalists and writers who, while very aware of what we are doing to the planet, are less focused on the loss of the Romantic sense of a transcendent wilderness and more interested in the way we may actually carry "nature" around inside us. Nature for them is not "other", not just out there, as it is for many people. The crisis of the Anthropocene is due to our lack of understanding that we are a part of nature, rather than apart from it. We have evolved from this planet and have failed to see that we – human nature and human society – are continuing to evolve with it.

One of the new generation of science journalists is Gaia Vince whose remarkable *Adventures in the Anthropocene: a Journey to the Heart of the Planet We Made* (2014) won the Royal Society Winton Prize for Science Books. She was the first woman ever to win the prize. Vince left her desk at the much-respected *Nature* journal and set off to meet people out in the new nature – McKibben's *Eaarth*. In *Adventures* she writes imaginatively about the history and make-up of the planet and, with an instinctive and realistic optimism, records the ingenious and poignant creativity of human beings across the world struggling to adjust to the unprecedented dangers of the Anthropocene we in the Western world have brought into being.

Vince describes the extreme impoverishment and suffering

she finds everywhere, but in her odyssean adventures she also meets a whole anthropocenean, internetted community of inspired entrepreneurs. There is, for instance, Chewang Norphel, the retired railway engineer in Ladakh – "The Glacierman" – who created an artificial glacier, enabling an eco-system to support a number of local villages, and thereby providing a model for wider application in the developing world. Or Salomon Parco and friends in Peru who, aggrieved at the "black rocky summit" left by the retreat of their local glacier, have started painting the mountain white, on the principle that white reflects heat and is more likely to keep the mountain cool enough for ice to form. Of course, as an academic glaciologist who has been studying Peru's glaciers for some forty years, pointed out, it is hardly feasible to paint the whole Andean chain white, but Parco's quixotic and ingenious initiative may buy some time for the local community and lead to further thinking about man-made water-storage enterprises. Gaia Vince retains her faith in the ingenuity of the human species.

Vince is an articulate and creative example of an increasing number of people who have a new awareness of the Earth and our place on it. This is a true global consciousness, based not solely in economic or rational Enlightenment concepts but crucially also in ethical and aesthetic values, as well as scientific ones. If the Anthropocene is truly "The Age of Humans" and the Earth is now the human planet, then the crucial question remains: are we doomed to be a destructive – and self-destructive – species or can we learn to be responsible, even at this late stage?

The answer to this question depends on our knowledge of ourselves. Could it be that, ironically, we can come to know ourselves only when we, and all life around us, are now most at risk? Interestingly, Vince's next book, yet to be published by Penguin, is *Cultural Being: The Science of our History (or how Adam bit the snake)* , "an original and scientific take on humanity's evolution" which, according also to the publisher's information, "looks back to 40,000 years ago when humankind invented culture to free itself from a 'simply reactive relationship' with the physical matter of the Earth".

"A Time to Leap"

The classical evolutionists thought in terms of gradual, geological change over vast eons of time. But that doesn't account for the rapidity of the recent shift from the Holocene to the Anthropocene. Later thinkers have conjectured that evolution sometimes makes leaps. Steven Jay Gould and Niles Eldredge called this "punctuated equilibrium", in reference to biological evolution. When the processes of nature reach a tipping point there can be a dramatic change, a reversal that occurs quickly – instantly in geological time. This might help explain the five great evolutionary extinctions in the Earth's history preceding the sixth taking place now. Given our tardiness in helping ourselves today it is thought that only a cultural "leap" can rescue us from the catastrophe that awaits.

Naomi Klein has written about the need for a leap in the last chapter of *No Is Not Enough*, "A Time to Leap". The Canadian NDP has even published their *Leap Manifesto – a Call for a Canada Based on Caring for the Earth and One Another* (which grew out of a two-day gathering in Toronto in May 2015 and is printed as a postscript in Klein's book). But I would like to suggest that a "leap" is not just something we intentionally make or "do", in the usual sense of this. It's also a response to changes that appear to go on beyond our control, call it evidence of "God's invisible hand" or the directional spirit of evolution beyond the ability of the human intellect alone to comprehend. For us to make an adequate response requires us to call on capacities within ourselves we have neglected in our modern age. To get an idea of what these might be it may help to step outside the usual parameters of modern Western culture and the dismaying split between science and the humanities.

The Wheel of Dharma

It is difficult for many people to know how how their individual lives can be an adequate response to the planetary crisis. In the East they have a word for an ethical practice which a person follows in all situations, however hopeless. It is called *dharma,* and "dharma practice" is what an individual person takes refuge in. It is personal to each individual. *Dharma* is a central notion in both the Hindu and Buddhist traditions. The word literally means "carrying" or "holding". In the Hindu tradition it is a comprehensive term and refers to what determines our true essence. As the basis of all human morality and ethics, it is the lawful order of the universe and the foundation of all religion. Hindus think of it as *sanatana-dharma* – the eternal religion. Personal dharma can be more effective when joined to social and universal dharma.

In the Buddhist tradition it also has a number of meanings. It points to the cosmic law, the "great norm" underlying our world, but also refers to the teachings of the Buddha, who recognised and formulated this "law". His is the teaching that expresses the universal truth. These are not just the teachings of the historical Shakyamuni, or Siddhartha Gautama Buddha but those which emerged after Gautama and which constitute the developing tradition. It is said that the teachings evolve by "the turning of the wheel of dharma". These "turnings" could be said to be the "leap" in the spiralling dynamic we know as evolution. Two and a half millennia ago Gautama Buddha turned the first wheel, but there was a second and a third in the early centuries of the first millennium CE.

The evolution of Buddhism

The first turning of the wheel was the practical, therapeutic and ethical teachings of the historical individual Gautama Buddha, with particular emphasis on the issue of suffering and its cessation. The second came in the second century CE with the teaching of the great "middle way" Indian sage, Nagarjuna – "the second buddha" – and his subtle exposition of the truth of the emptiness of all things, including ourselves. We could speculate that the spirit of his teachings are echoed in the quantum revolution in the early years of twentieth century physics.

The third Turning is considered the teachings on the nature of mind and consciousness of the *Yogachara* – "Mind Only" – school of Asanga and Vasubandhu in India in the fifth century. These "turnings" are like major waves of enlightenment and are said to emerge in times of great need. Again these teachings are echoed in our current focus on the subject of consciousness – the "hard problem" of today – whether in the scientific interests of neurological science or the more subjective focus of mindfulness and meditation.

Some think a "fourth turning" is now happening, but as a global phenomenon not just a "Buddhist" one, though Buddhism is an important element in it. It is more the integration of all the great historical traditions, including Shamanism and the many aboriginal ways, Hinduism, Daoism, Buddhism, Judaism, Christianity and Islam, but also embracing the secular science and humanities of the West. Some people even think that, despite – or partly because of – the ecological emergency we are causing, we now may be at the same time entering a period of cultural renewal similar to the emergence of great intellectual and spiritual enlightenment across the world in the middle centuries of the first Millennium BCE, which the German historian and philosopher, Karl Jaspers, has called "The Axial Age", and which Karen Armstrong has written about in *The Great Transformation: The World in the Time of Buddha, Socrates, Confucius and Jeremiah* (2006).

The three historical Buddhist turnings of the wheel of dharma emerged in the development of Indian Buddhism in the 1200 years between 600 BCE and 600 CE. After the Muslim invasions of India in the twelfth century *buddha dharma*, which had already spread along the Silk Road to the Far East of China, Korea and Japan, migrated to "the roof of the world", Tibet – 'the land of snows" – where it was developed and refined in relative isolation for a thousand years. The "wheel" may have continued slowly rotating but there were no major revolutions, though this is disputed by some scholars. Certainly, Tibetan thought and practice continued to translate and evolve the profound teachings of India and integrate them with the traditions of its own indigenous Bon religion.

The turning of the wheel as a philosophical and cultural evolutionary phenomenon is really part of a spiral. The wheel turns, spins, or revolves, in one historical context, then it could be said to rest a while before turning, or spiralling, again, in a different historical context, also at a different level. The spirit of the teachings may be seen to arise, but in a new and developed form. The sacred writings and thought of Buddhism, for instance, and the Indian Vedanta tradition began to be known and read about in the Western world only in the nineteenth century, although it was not until the twentieth that Chinese Chan and Japanese Zen Buddhism reached the West. And, then, only in the second half of the century did the Tibetan diaspora – resulting from the Chinese invasion of Tibet in the 1950s and 60s – promise to bring a greater clarity to our understanding of the second and third turnings of the dharma wheel – the teachings on emptiness and consciousness.

The Tibetan diaspora

While this migration west was a major challenge for the Buddhist traditions, many have also seen it as potentially leading to a much-needed renewal of secular modernity. Jeffrey Paine's book, *Re-enchantment: Tibetan Buddhism Comes to the West (2004),* for instance gives a fascinating account of this chapter in Tibet's history. The Chinese invaded Tibet in the late nineteen fifties and early sixties. They killed over a million Tibetans, many of them monks, and destroyed thousands of monasteries in the name of modernity. The Dalai Lama led the movement of exiled lamas over the Himalayas where he eventually set up his headquarters and government – in – exile in Dharamsala in Northern India. From here the Tibetan teaching diaspora has spread across the world. While in the Middle Ages Buddhism moved east from India at walking and camel pace along the Silk Road to China, Mongolia, Tibet, and Japan, it now travels by jet throughout Europe, the Americas, and the rest of the world.

As Jeffrey Paine recounts in his introductory chapter, "A Thousand Years in the Eye of God", there was a remarkable conjunction of medieval monks and the young generation in 'sixties America. Wondering what they were going to do with themselves after their expulsion from Tibet the lamas in exile, who had grown up never knowing or hearing of America, began lecturing and actually attracting American students by the hundreds and the thousands and, as Paine writes,

> To win a place in the modern world those Tibetans had to cross a thousand years of religious development and do it in double time. In effect they recapitulated the history of religion....in a single generation. Nothing

quite like this has happened before, and with no other religions left intact, nothing like it will happen ever again.

As Joseph Campbell put it: "If a European scholar – monk of the period of, say, Abelard, were to appear in today's New York....the miracle would be scarcely more remarkable or important for the students of political and religious history." The same might now also be said of the students of the other humanities, including psychology. The historian, Arnold Toynbee, declared: "The coming of Buddhism to the West may well prove to be the most important event of the twentieth century", and Einstein, in reflecting that religion will have to cope with modern scientific needs in the future and should "transcend a personal God and avoid dogma and theology", believed that Buddhism answered this description.

Toynbee and Einsteins' remarks suggest that the phenomenon of the spread of Buddhist teachings is a significant historical and cultural event for the modern world. In fact there is now a body of Western – born Tibetan speakers, translators, commentators, and teachers who in the last twenty years or so have contributed to a proliferation of books published on the Tibetan dharma – translations of increasing numbers of sutras and tantras (sacred writings) in Tibetan – many themselves, very accurate translations from Sanskrit texts that are no longer extant – and accompanying commentaries. These are new to the West and are now easily available through a number of dedicated publishers. The Tibetan lamas, themselves, observing the disenchanted condition of modern Western society, but also sensing the opportunity, given our high level of education and intellectual curiosity, have responded energetically to the demand world – wide for their teachings.

Enlightenment in a new Axial Age

The notion of a "fourth turning" and the growing sense that, despite our gross materialism, we are living in a new axial age makes this potentially a very significant time to be living – for the tradition of Buddhism as well as ourselves in the West. Buddhism is the one 'religion' not intimidated by western science. It has much to teach us. At the same time it has much to learn, not only from our natural but also from our human sciences. Ken Wilber makes this the theme of his recent major work *The Religion of Tomorrow. A Vision of the Future of the Great Traditions* (2017). (This is a challenging book and he has followed it up with a shorter introductory summary of his ideas, entitled *Integral Buddhism and the future of Spirituality* (2018)). Again, as Wilber emphasises, although the idea of a fourth turning is taken from the Buddhist tradition, it is not exclusive to Buddhism but applies to the spirit of other traditions too. It is now a global, multicultural event, affecting the whole planet and all its traditions. This is in keeping with the systemic and integral vision which many people feel is central to the new awareness felt in many societies, cultures and religious, or spiritual, ways.

What Wilber also describes in his book – in a theoretical detail only he is, perhaps, capable of – are the two dimensions of enlightenment currently available to us today. One is the contemplative practice of WAKING UP (Wilber capitalises them for the sake of emphasis) a tradition known to most cultures in different forms in all human history but which we in the modern world have lost sight of. What the perennial traditions offer is an awakening to a sense of transcendence, the vertical dimension of experience, both depth and height.

The other dimension of enlightenment is GROWING UP, a recent development in modern Western culture. Natural science has revealed on the one hand how astonishing the physical universe is, while the European Enlightenment on the other amounted, in the title of one of the books of the historian of "the Radical Enlightenment", Jonathan Israel, to *A Revolution of the Mind* (2011). Science is responsible for the revolution in the way we view matter and life while Enlightenment thinking, with its radical new human values of liberty, equality and fraternity, created a potential ethical revolution in the human and mind sciences, with implications particularly for political, social and civic life.

In Wilber's view, what makes this a unique age is that, for the first time in the world's evolution, these two – Waking Up and Growing Up – can be combined in a new enlightenment. In the West we are awakening to an ultimate reality we have lost sight of while traditional cultures, which have tended to be authoritarian or theocratic, are being challenged by the developmental and evolutionary sciences which have emerged in the modern West. A fourth turning would entail the integration of these two modes of enlightenment.

Waking up

There are many paths to coming to know, or realise, who we essentially are. We have lost touch, for instance, with the more subtle levels of consciousness that constitute our true nature, a nature that persists through all the states of waking, dreaming and dreamless sleep we live through every day and night of our lives. The secret heart of us might even be something formless, the source and cause of our being. And a knowledge of this could transform our relationship to all the suffering and heartache we experience in our daily, waking lives.

It is what Richard Maurice Bucke has called, in the title of his classic book, our *Cosmic Consciousness: A Study in the Evolution of the Human Mind* (1901).How we recover this awareness, this perennial wisdom, is, perhaps, as important as meeting the challenge of climate change. In fact the two are essentially related since the one may well come from the absence of the other.

If we had not forgotten who we are we might not be facing the climate crisis. The Tibetans teach that four contemplations or "thoughts that turn the mind" are the essential basis of any path to wisdom or awakening. In *Indestructible Truth: The Living Spirituality of Tibetan Buddhism*, the first of his recent and readable two volumes, *The History of Tibetan Buddhism* (2002) Reginald Ray, their author, following the lead of Chogyam Trungpa, refers to them as "the four reminders".

The four reminders

> The precious opportunities and
> endowments are rare and easily
> destroyed. The world and its inhabitants
> are impermanent; soon, I too will die.
> Without fail my good and bad deeds
> will ripen in me, And there is no lasting
> happiness within samsara –
> cyclic existence.
> **Jamgon Kongtrul**

The first reminder points to the precious opportunity that is given to us all as a result of being born as a human being, an opportunity that can be taken away at any time. It is a crucial irony that, just at the time in human history when we have put the world at risk, we have also discovered how mysterious, complex and beautiful it is. Just as science has made our extinction possible it also reveals to us something of the preciousness of life and of the limitless possibilities of the universe we inhabit. Who doesn't wonder this when we watch David Attenborough's extraordinary programmes? We glimpse the magic all around us, it seems, only when we may be on the point of saying goodbye to it.

The second reminds us that all life is impermanent, including our own, and that we can lose it at any moment. As we contemplate the climate crisis we are also forced to acknowledge our essential transience. While we know that death comes to us all as individuals at any time, we can now conceive of our species death too. We may begin to wonder if there is anything necessary, or ordained, about our existence. Despite all our achievements, are we not as impermanent, and as contingent, as any other life form? Was it ever otherwise?

The third insists that nothing happens without a reason and an effect and that all our thoughts and actions have positive or negative consequences. We have to acknowledge we have brought about the possibility of our own destruction. We cannot blame it on some supernatural power or pretend, like the ancient Greeks, that we are the victims of the Gods. "As ye sow, so shall ye reap" is the great Christian expression of the Eastern doctrine of karma. There are no actions and no thoughts without consequences, good or bad. We simply cannot escape this. It is our delusion that we think we can. Whatever the future brings us in this century, it is we who are responsible. Of course, with regard to karma, we can sow creative seeds as well as negative ones. "Growing up" may help us to acknowledge this and act responsibly rather than destructively.

The fourth reminder, or "thought that turns the mind", tells us that true happiness is to be found by looking beyond the cycle of birth and death, beyond what in Sanskrit is called samsara. It dawns on us that, just as we see how the very life cycle - the process of birth and death, time itself - can come to an end, we have to wonder, despite all our science, whether we have even begun to understand it. Perhaps there is another way of looking at life that we have missed. Are the processes of birth and death quite what they seem or are there secrets that lie within them - beyond the arising and dissolving of life or the mystery of past, present and future – that only now we begin to discern? Is the world, and the life it supports, including ourselves, now becoming transparent to us in a way we could not have dreamed?

Growing up

The fourth reminder, or "thought that turns the mind", refers to the notion of samsara, the cycle of birth and death. Traditional paths of waking up have emphasised the need to escape the material world of samsara and thereby attain its opposite, nirvana – heaven rather than earth. In the modern

West we are sceptical of this practice. Samsara – the world of becoming, of transience – may bring pain and suffering but it is also sublimely beautiful. Why escape it? Perhaps there is a way of living within it. The Eastern split between samsara and nirvana feels a bit like the orthodox Christian theological separation of heaven and hell, or this world and the next.

The poet, William Blake, wrote prophetically of *The Marriage of Heaven and Hell* – for "hell" we could now read "earth". "Roses" he declared "are planted where thorns grow, and on the barren heath sing the honey bees". "Without contraries" he continued "is no progression. Attraction and repulsion, reason and energy, love and hate are necessary to human existence". Good and evil, heaven and hell, are the two principles that lead to "progression". For Blake "Energy is eternal delight" and the restraint of desire can be at a cost.

In separating the "contraries" of body and soul we introduce suffering into the world and have traditionally called it "evil" – "the voice of the devil". But the truth is, in Blake's words: "1. Man has no body distinct from his soul. For that called body is a portion of the soul discerned by the five senses, the chief inlets of soul in this age.

2. Energy is the only life, and is from the body; and reason is the bound and outward circumference of energy.

3. Energy is eternal delight."

Blake illustrated the problem of the separation of heaven and hell by reference to the poet, John Milton. When Milton wrote his great epic *Paradise Lost*, "Satan" was the hero of the poem, really the Messiah. Blake famously noted: "The reason Milton wrote in fetters when he wrote of angels and God, and at Liberty when of devils and hell, is because he was a true poet, and of the devil's party without knowing it". For us, perhaps, Blake was also saying that we neglect to examine our shadow at our peril. "The Proverbs of Hell" are the great aphoristic lines of English poetry. They convey the essence of wisdom. Blake is not denying the truth of "Heaven" but insisting that the world is a "marriage" of them both. Without hell, there is no real heaven. He lamented our splitting of them.

The discovery of the power of reason and the Enlightenment aspiration towards the human values of liberty, equality and fraternity were a step in cultural evolution and surely a sign of "growing up", something to be welcomed and developed. But as the historian, Norman Hampson, reminded us in

The Enlightenment (1968) while the 18th century brought in "A New Heaven and Earth", it also gave the age "Not Peace but a Sword". The Heaven of Reason has its price. Enlightenment comes with a shadow.

I have been reading Steven Pinker's *Enlightenment NOW: the Case for Reason, Science, Humanism and Progress* (2018), which applauds the achievements of modernity and suggests we have forgotten "to appreciate progress and the ideals that make it possible". Yes, Pinker makes a case and argues against "progressophobia". We take the science of modernity for granted.

But he neglects to explore its shadow. John Gray's *Enlightenment's Wake: Politics and culture at the close of the modern age* may have been published in 1995, six years after the fall of the Berlin Wall when the "end of history" was declared – along with the global supremacy of liberal Enlightenment's values - but it was only six years before 9/11 and another seven before the global financial collapse of 2008. "The Enlightenment project" – a phrase implying criticism – refers not so much to the 18th century Enlightenment itself as to the translation of its values and ideals uncritically into the modern age. Gray's skepticism about modern "progress" highlights our failure to take an evolutionary perspective on Western liberalism, which, with its mutated form, neo-liberalism, is ripe for transformation. Where, then, might we look for an evolutionary perspective in this twenty-first century?

Cultural evolution

In his book, *Evolutionaries: Unlocking the Spiritual and Cultural Potential of Science's Greatest Idea* (2012), Carter Phipps describes a movement of visionary scientists, philosophers and spiritual thinkers who are responsible for a new understanding of evolution. These men and women, who integrate science and culture with an awareness of the more subtle forms of consciousness, he calls "evolutionaries". They are really true revolutionaries who understand we live in a "sociable cosmos" where cooperation and unity is contextual to conflict.

Phipps identifies the sense in which the spirit of evolution has directionality - teleology - (as opposed to the modern idea of progress) and creativity - Bergson's great idea. It also has the power to raise human nature above and beyond itself. By realising we are, in the words of Julian Huxley, "Evolution become conscious of itself", we can find ourselves transformed. Phipps explores the developing worldview of cultural evolution in the history of philosophers such as Hegel, Bergson and Whitehead and through conversations with many contemporary thinkers, but he also points to two major figures in the last century, one from the West and one from the East.

Two significant "evolutionaries"

Teilhard de Chardin (1881-1955) was the great Christian visionary who wrote the extraordinary *Le Phenomene Humaine* (Written in 1937, published posthumously 1955) and originally translated as *The Phenomenon of Man* (tr. by Bernard Wall, 1959) but more accurately as *The Human Phenomenon* (tr. by Sarah Appleton-Weber (1999)). Teilhard was a French idealist philosopher and Jesuit priest but also a palaeontologist and geologist.

His writings on evolution were not accepted by the Catholic Church. They were banned while he was alive and he himself was sent to work far away in China. But his teachings have become more widely known and acknowledged for their importance since his death. Even Bishop Michael Curry mentioned him admiringly in his spirited address at the royal wedding of Harry and Megan in St. George's Windsor Chapel this year.

Reading Teilhard is not easy, for he writes, as it were, on the largest possible canvas - a geological scale - not just from a scientific but also from a human existential perspective. Reading him is a bit like reading Ken Wilber. He introduces us to a cosmic dimension, which our modern intellects find disconcerting, more comfortable are we with smaller-scale human detail. But he is interested to explore the central vital question that scientific geologists and earth scientists don't ask - and which stumped Sigmund Freud when he allowed himself to think about it: how did life emerge from matter, and how did consciousness emerge from life? And, of course, what comes after purely human consciousness?

For Teilhard, evolution, as the vital force he conceives it, makes sense of the universe. "Complexification" – the involutionary force - is at the heart of creation and is responsible for the evolution of matter into a geosphere, then into a biosphere, before becoming consciousness (humanity) and ultimately - being the Christian he was - into supreme consciousness – his "omega point". Humanity was not so much "man" in his own right but the expression of a planetised "noosphere" – mind sphere – much like the biosphere is the life sphere. Hence his emphasis on the collective consciousness of the human phenomenon. The omega point is presumably when we realise our identity with the earth and the universe it lives in.

The other significant figure – from the East – was Sri Aurobindo (1872-1950), an Indian philosopher, yogi, poet and nationalist. In his younger days he was active in the India movement for independence from British rule, but during a spell in prison he underwent an experience of enlightenment, thereafter devoting his life to his vision of human progress and spiritual evolution.

He may be known as an Indian spiritual leader – author of many works on yoga and sacred Indian writings, and who inspired an ashram in Poona of worldwide renown - but he had received a humanistic education in England throughout his childhood and young adult years (including study at Cambridge) and was strongly influenced by Western thought. As a result he was not uncritical of the classical yoga systems of Hinduism which he thought offered a one-sided "ascent" to the "divine".

In *The Future Evolution of Man*, subtitled *The Divine Life upon Earth* (1963, edited by P. B. Sainte-Hilaire) is a brief compilation of Aurobindo's voluminous writings, including

The Life Divine, his major work, concerning his thoughts about evolution. Darwin, of course, had given expression in *The Origin of the Species* to evolution as a biological phenomenon.

Aurobindo, born into a cultural background of classical Indian idealism, thought in terms of the evolution of consciousness. Despite his exploration of the material world, man also aspired to know absolute "pure truth". In *The Future Evolution* Saint-Hilaire summarises Aurobindo's conception of evolution:

> Life evolves out of Matter, Mind out of
> Life, because they are already involved
> there: Matter is a form of veiled Life, Life
> a form of veiled Mind. May not Mind be a
> form and veil of a higher power, the Spirit,
> which would be supramental in its nature?
> Man's highest aspiration would then only
> indicate the gradual unveiling of the Spirit
> within, the preparation of a higher life
> upon earth.
> **"Summary" p vi**

In *The Life Divine* Sri Aurobindo described the "supramental" dimension of mind beyond the reach of the normal and subtle levels of human nature but which were accessible through a path of what he called "integral yoga". As he explained in *Letters on Yoga*:

> men have tried to reach it (the supramental) by raising themselves up to it; what was not attained was a method to integrate it into one's life". His integral yoga enabled the "descent" of this divine supramental into the material world we daily inhabit. Thus it was possible to make space for a superhuman consciousness - what he called "supermind" - within our normal human consciousness.

Interestingly there are parallels between the worldview of Teilhard and Sri Aurobindo: both had an expanded view of cosmic as well as human history; both had an experience of a consciousness beyond the normal human mind; both are idealists but with a grounding in materialist thought - Teilhard, a geologist by training, Sri Aurobindo, educated in Western thinking; both were convinced of the importance of evolution in making sense of the universe, not just as a biological process but also as a cultural phenomenon.

Climate change: challenge and opportunity

On the opening information page of Mike Hulme's book *Why We Disagree About Climate Change: Understanding Controversy, Inaction and Opportunity* (2009), it states:

> Climate change is not a 'problem' waiting for a 'solution'. It is an environmental, cultural and political phenomenon which is reshaping the way we think about ourselves, our societies and humanity's place on Earth.

Mike Hulme is Professor of Climate Change in the School of Environmental Services at the University of East Anglia in the U.K. and founding Director of the Tyndall Centre for Climate Change Research.

In the preface to his book he presents climate change as an "idea" as much as a physical phenomenon that can be observed and measured. It is now "a social phenomenon" and our cultural, social, political and ethical practices are reinterpreting what it means. In the book he examines "this mutating idea", seeing how from the different perspectives - "depending who one is and where one stands" - the unfolding idea of climate change means different things to different people and implies different courses of action.

The story of climate change is not one that begins in ignorance and ends in certainty. It is "much more interesting than that". It is a story about "the meeting of Nature and Culture, and about how humans are central actors in both of these realms, and about how we are continually creating and re-creating both Nature and Culture". In his book Hulme reframes the question. We should ask ourselves not just what we can do about the climate emergency but how it changes us.

Climate change is known to be a "wicked - or super-wicked - problem", as opposed to a finite "tame problem", susceptible to a scientific solution. It is an open-ended issue, an "idea" that changes with our thinking about it. Einstein famously said "we cannot solve our problems with the same thinking we used when we created them".

But climate change requires us to change more than our thinking. It is also an opportunity to explore who we essentially are, not just who we think we are but who we experience ourselves to be. This is the challenge and opportunity of the new Axial Age.

June 2018

References

Angus, Ian, *Facing the Anthropocene: Fossil Capitalism and the Crisis of the Earth System* (2016).

Aurobindo, Sri, *The Future Evolution of Man* (2002)

Batchelor, Stephen, *The Awakening of the West: the Encounter of Buddhism and the West* (2015, 2011)

Bateson, Gregory, *Steps to an Ecology of Mind*, (2000).

Blake, William, *The Marriage of Heaven and Hell* (1975)

————— *Auguries of Innocence* (1975)

Coates, Ta-Nehisi, "We should have seen Trump Coming", *Guardian*, (Sept. 29, 2019).

Dalai Lama, *The Universe in a Single Atom* (2007)

Dodds, Joseph, *Psychoanalysis and Ecology at the Edge of Chaos: Complexity Theory, Deleuze/Guattari and Psychoanalysis for a Climate in Crisis*, (2011)

Eagleton, Terry, *Culture and the Death of God* (2015)

Easwaran, Eknath, *The Upanishads* (1987, 2007)

Eddington , Arthur, *The Nature of the Physical World* (1928, 2012)

Emerson, Ralph Waldo, "The Over-Soul" in *Nature and Selected Essays* (2003)

Gebser, Jean, *The Ever-Present Origin*, translated by Barstad and Mickunas (1986)

Godman, David, *Be As You Are: the Teachings of Sri Ramana Maharshi* (1991)

Gray, John, *Enlightenment's Wake: Politics and Culture at the Close of the Modern Age*, (2007, 1997)

————— *Al Qaeda and What It Means to be Modern* (2005)

Haidt, Jonathan, "When and Why Nationalism Beats Globalism", *The American Interest,* (10 July, 2016)

Hamilton, Clive, *Requiem for a Species* (2010)

————— *Defiant Earth: the Fate of Humans in the Anthropocene* (2017)

Hulme, Mike, *Why We Disagree about Climate Change – Understanding Controversy, Inaction, and Opportunity* (2007)

Jaspers, Karl, *The Origin and Goal of History* (2011, 1953)

Kingsnorth, Paul, "The Four Degrees", *London Review of Books*,
(23 October, 2014)
———— *Guardian*, "The lie of the land: does environmentalism
have a future in the age of Trump?" (18 March, 2017)
Klein, Naomi, *This Changes Everything: Capitalism vs. the Climate* (2014)
———— *No Is Not Enough: Defeating the New Shock Politics* (2018)
Koyre, Alexander, *From the Closed World to the Infinite Universe* (2016, 1957)
Lear, Jonathan, *A Case for Irony* (2011)
———— *Radical Hope: Ethics in the Face of Cultural Devastation* (2008)
Leavis, F.R., *The Two Cultures* (2012, 1962)
Marshall, George, *Don't Even Think About It –
Why Our Brains Are Wired to Ignore Climate Change* (2015)
McKibben, Bill, *The End of Nature* (1990)
———— *Eaarth: Making a Life on a Tough New Planet* (2011)
———— *The Comforting Whirlwind: God, Job, and the Scale of Creation*
(2005)
Mishra, Pankaj, *Age of Anger* (2018)
———— *An End to Suffering: the Buddha in the World* (2004)
———— "Welcome to the Age of Anger", *Guardian*,
(December 8, 2016)
Monbiot, George, "How Do We Get Out of this Mess?
Guardian, (September 11, 2017)
Montaigne, *The Complete Essays*, translated by M.A.Screech, (1993)
Nisargadatta, Sri, Maharaj, *I Am That: talks with SNM*, translated from the
Marathi tape recordings by Maurice Frydman, (1973, 2015)
Paine, Jeffrey, *Re-Enchantment: Tibetan Buddhism Comes to the West* (2005)
Phipps, Carter, *Evolutionaries: Unlocking the Spiritual and Cultural
Potential of Science's Greatest Idea* (2012)
Pinker, Steven, *Enlightenment Now: the Case for Reason, Science,
Humanism and Progress* (2019)
Plotinus, *The Enneads*, translated by Stephen MacKenna (1956)
Prigogine, Illya & Stengers, Isabelle, *Order Out of Chaos*, (1984)
Ramana Maharshi, *The Spiritual Teachings of R M*, (1972)
———— *Talks With Ramana Maharshi*, (2000-2010)

Rose, Jacqueline, "Introduction" in Freud,
  modern Penguin classics, general editor, Adam Phillips,
  Mass Psychology and Other Writings (2004)
Rust, Mary-Jane, and Totten, Nick, editors, *Vital Signs: Psychological
  Responses to Ecological Crisis*, (2012)
Samuels, Andrew, *Political Psyche* (1993)
————— *Plural Psyche* (1989)
Samuels, Andrew, et al, *Critical Dictionary of Jungian Analysis* (1986)
Schumacher, Ernst, *Guide for the Perplexed* (1977)
Secret of Golden Flower, translated by Thomas Cleary (1991)
Simms, Andrew, *We Are More Than This: Coleridge lecture* (2016)
Solnit, Rebecca, *A Paradise Built in Hell* (2009)
Soeng Mu, *The Heart of the Universe: exploring the Heart Sutra* (2010.)
Spinoza, Benedict, *Ethics*, edited by Stuart Hampshire, (1996)
Teilhard, de Chardin, *The Human Phenomenon*
  translated by Sarah Appleton-Weber (2021)
Underhill, Evelyn, *Mysticism* (1990, 1911)
————— *Practical Mysticism* (2011, 1914)
Vince, Gaia, *Adventures in the Anthropocene – A Journey to the Heart of the
  Planet We Made* (2014)
Weintrobe, Sally, editor, *Engaging With Climate Change: Psychoanalytic and
  Interdisciplinary Perspectives*, (2013)
Wilber, Ken, editor, *Quantum Questions: Mystical Writings of the World's
  Greatest Physicists* (2001, 1984)
————— *A Brief History of Everything* (2017, 1996)
————— *A Theory of Everything: An Integral Vision for Business, Politics,
  Science, and Spirituality* (2000)
————— *No Boundary: Eastern and Western Approaches to Personal Growth*
  (2001, 1984)
————— *The Future of Religion: A Vision for the Future of the Great Traditions* (2018)
————— *Integral Buddhism and the Future of Spirituality* (2018)
————— *Trump and a Post-Truth World* (2017)
Wordsworth, William, *Lines written a Few Miles Above Tintern Abbey*, (1898)
Yeats, W.B. and Shri Purohit Swami, *The Upanishads*, (1937)

Index

Tony Cartwright has always been interested in the integration of our dynamic Western culture with the timeless wisdom and contemplative practices of the East. He has also been involved in Green politics since the Eighties. His professional career was in mental health, first as a social worker and then as a family group and systemic psychotherapist in an adult psychotherapy service. He is now retired and spends his time thinking and writing about the global challenges of our age. He has been affiliated to the UK Climate Psychology Alliance since its inception some ten years ago. Further, and more recent, writings are available on his personal website: **www.thetimelessaxis.com**.

Printed in Great Britain
by Amazon

11282638R00120